Secrets of the Resilient Empath

Protect Your Energy & Cultivate Your Gifts as a Highly Sensitive Person

Jennifer Lauren Parker

Copyright © 2021, Jennifer Lauren Parker

Published in the United States by Quantum Heart Publishing, Dallas, Georgia

Cover Art by Paula Ambrosio

All rights reserved. No part of this publication may be reproduced, distributed, or transmitted in any form or by any means, including photocopying, recording, or other electronic or mechanical methods, without the prior written permission of the publisher, except in the case of brief quotations embodied in reviews and certain other non-commercial uses permitted by copyright law.

Identifiers:

ISBN: 979-8-9854352-0-7 (paperback)

ISBN: 979-8-9854352-1-4 (e-book)

ISBN: 979-8-9854352-2-1 (hardback)

Library of Congress Control Number: 2021924748

Disclaimer:

Although the author has made every effort to ensure that the information in this book was correct at press time, and while this publication is designed to provide accurate information in regard to the subject matter covered, the author assumes no responsibility for errors, inaccuracies, omissions, or any other inconsistencies herein and hereby disclaim any liability to any party for any loss, damage, or disruption caused by errors or omissions, whether such errors or omissions result from negligence, accident, or any other cause.

This publication is meant as a source of valuable information for the reader, however it is not meant as a substitute for direct expert assistance. If such a level of assistance is required, the services of a competent professional should be sought.

Contents

Dedication	V
Is this book for you?	VI
1. Chapter 1 Not Weak, Not Alone	1
2. Chapter 2 Being A Highly Sensitive Human	8
3. Chapter 3 Elephants	13
4. Chapter 4 The Gifts of Sensitivity	23
5. Chapter 5 The Science of Being an Empath	33
6. Chapter 6 Inside the Highly Sensitive Mind	47
7. Chapter 7 Resilience & Reframing	55
8. Chapter 8	68

Anxiety & Overwhelm

9. Chapter 9
   Life, Breath, and the PNS — 78

10. Chapter 10
    No and Yes — 90

11. Chapter 11
    People Problems — 106

12. Chapter 12
    The Narcissist Factor — 120

13. Chapter 13
    Trusting Yourself — 130

14. Chapter 14
    Socks & Swampmonsters — 142

15. Chapter 15
    Four Tricks — 154

16. Chapter 16
    Resilience 2.0 — 164

17. Chapter 17
    Three Secret Keys — 176

A note before you go... — 185

Acknowledgements — 186

About the Author — 188

To my family who lets me be my gentle but stubbornly strong-willed self.

Is this book for you?

Some of us have been born without a standard-issue filter between us and the world. We experience life deeply, noticing little things others miss and absorbing the energy and emotions that pulsate around us.

There are certain gifts that come with this high sensitivity, but plenty of struggles as well. After all, it's hard to maintain our own energy and set boundaries when we sponge up the emotions of others. Since we are living in a tough world where fast, tangible productivity is highly valued, we may have taken on the feeling that the things we excel at (understanding others, thinking deeply, being creative) are not important. Too often, highly sensitive people and empaths struggle to thrive in a world that doesn't feel like it was made for us.

All of this might make us feel weak, but the truth is we are anything but. We all have the capacity for resilience in us, but sometimes we aren't sure how to access it. This book will help you uncover the secret to unlocking your own resilience.

This starts with seeing the value you bring to the table and reclaiming the gifts you were blessed with. As you read on, you'll be guided through practical ways of setting boundaries, building inner strength, and managing energy so you can do the work you were meant to do.

Now more than ever, we need people who have deep empathy for other humans, animals, and the planet. We need creatives and visionaries to shine a light on what else is possible. The goal of this book is to empower highly sensitive empaths to live fully into their gifts, no matter how tough the world around us gets.

So, is this book for you? If you think it might be, I hope you'll read on. But before you get started, I have a gift for you. Go to jenniferlaurenparker.com and grab a free download of The Resilient Empath Journal. In it you'll find journaling prompts and exercises to help you get the most out of the lessons ahead. Enjoy!

Chapter 1

Not Weak, Not Alone

"We have not journeyed all this way because we are made of sugar candy." --- Winston S. Churchill

"Toughen up, kid." Have you heard that one? I don't know about you, but the words give me flashbacks to shiny wooden floors, the smell of sweaty socks, and a teacher grimly shaking her head with a whistle gritted between her teeth. Knowing me, I was probably feigning illness in hopes of escaping to the nurse's office—or better yet, home.

If you were a sensitive and empathic kid, athletic or not, you probably got the message early in life that *toughness* is the cultural ideal. Feelings? Sorry, the world doesn't stop for crybabies. You're just *too sensitive*. Suck it up.

And so we end up here, feeling more than a little inadequate. We wonder why the business of life seems harder for us than most.

Deep down, we probably know we are smart—maybe even really intelligent. After all, our brains are always lit up, noticing everything, bubbling with imagination and ideas. But for Pete's sake, why do we freeze up at the most important moments? And why are the simplest things so draining? Like, should I really need a nap after going to Costco?

(The answer is yes, by the way. Everyone who braves Costco has earned a nap. Particularly if you go on a Friday at lunchtime, and all the more so if you encounter someone like the lady who yelled at me for taking too much time at the long underwear display.)

If some or all of this sounds familiar, you may be a **highly sensitive person** (HSP, for short). High sensitivity is an inborn trait discovered by psychologist Dr. Elaine Aron and described in her 1996 book, *The Highly Sensitive Person*. Since you picked up this book, you're quite likely to be a special version of an HSP: an empath.

Just in case no one has filled you in yet, an **empath** is a person who understands the thoughts and feelings of others more than is usual. This includes being highly sensitive to the energy of those around them. As we go on, we'll clarify how and why some of us are like this.

First things to know for those who are fuzzy on the details: all empaths are highly sensitive. Not all highly sensitive people are empaths. We'll be using both terms throughout the book and there will be many things that will apply to people across the spectrum of sensitivity. If something applies to everyone on that spectrum, I'll just say "highly sensitive" or "HSP." High sensitivity is at the root of being an empath, so we'll start there and then branch out. Much of the book will encompass the broader experience of HSPs, while a few chapters will resonate more specifically with empaths.

Oh, and one more thing: a lot of us are not big fans of these labels. Some don't like the word "sensitive" because it makes us sound weak, which we're definitely not. Others (me included) don't love the term "empath" because it just sounds plain weird. I'm different enough without odd descriptions taking me further into left field.

Still, I'm using these words because people are familiar with them, and I'm just not up to inventing a new vocabulary. So don't get too hung up on labels or word meanings; just see if the lessons resonate with you. Fair enough?

Shortly after starting this book, I had second thoughts. You know how it goes—you come up with an idea, get excited about it, and then the little negative voice pops up saying, "Eh, are you sure about this?" My inner Negative Nelly relayed this story: "Dr. Aron already wrote the Bible on highly sensitive people. No one needs your mindless unprofessional drivel."

Did I mention my Negative Nelly is a jerk?

Anyway, feeling a little forlorn about the whole thing, I decided to browse Amazon for more books on highly sensitive people. You know what? There really aren't that many.

Dr. Aron estimates HSPs account for 15-20 percent of the population. That's a decent chunk, huh? And yet, most people have no idea that the trait even exists! Therefore, the highly sensitive are often left without resources tailored to our unique needs. All the while, we are labeled as awkward, anxious, flaky, overly emotional—need I go on?

It's true, sometimes we wonder if we *are* those things, because we don't know how else to explain our behavior. We've had these negative descriptions repeated ad nauseam throughout our lives; it's no wonder they become part of our identity. We question whether we have what it takes to be strong and resilient, or even if we're cut out for this world at all.

Wouldn't it be helpful if more of us knew *why* we don't fit in? Why do we get exhausted or worked up when others seem to effortlessly keep a steady energy? Why do we feel things so deeply, including other people's emotions? And better yet, wouldn't it be nice if other people understood us and were accommodating, particularly in the case of highly sensitive children?

Really, more people need to be aware that some of us are born with more sensitive nervous systems, and that *there is absolutely nothing wrong with us.*

So, here you find yourself realizing high sensitivity is indeed a thing. I imagine this may or may not be of any comfort. After all, the word *"sensitive"* is almost looked at with a bit of contempt. No one ever says it as a compliment, do they?

I mean, we don't often hear something like, "I love how you handled that situation with such sensitivity!" or "It's so great how sensitive you are. I wish I could be more of a softy myself!"

In fact, it's usually the opposite. Usually, the word "sensitive" is paired with another word: T-O-O.

Well, let me assure you: as a highly sensitive human, you are not "too" much or "too" little, or even "too" sensitive. And despite the cultural connotations of the word, being *sensitive* does not equal being weak or fragile.

Friend, you are not made of sugar candy, even if you sometimes feel like chocolate left in the sun. I feel it too, but trust me—we are made of *more* than that.

Before we go any further, maybe I should introduce myself. I'm going to tell you some of my own stories as we go on, and it feels a little awkward to do so without a proper introduction. My name is Jennifer. I can be sweet, but also have a salty streak, and I'm definitely not made of sugar candy. I've always been an old soul and now have a few gray hairs to match. I'm a better writer than a talker. My credentials for writing this book are highly unimpressive. I'm a researcher, an observer, and a learn-the-hard-way-er. I've studied behavioral patterns, self-sabotage, habit change, and trauma—some professionally, as a coach and an Aroma Freedom Technique practitioner.

But honestly, most of what I will share with you is what I have learned in my ongoing project of patching my own highly sensitive, empathic little self together.

I really like figuring out what makes us humans tick, and what holds us back from really ticking. One of my favorite things is seeing people get through their own muck and step into who they were made to be.

You see, whether the world recognizes it or not, *you already are who you were made to be.* You have an incredible gift that is so very needed.

Now, I realize you may not clearly see the purpose of being highly sensitive at the moment. You may not see yourself in a great light at all, for one reason or another. It's OK. Remember this: *your potential is not defined by your current circumstances.* In other words, you've got a lot more inside of you than you can imagine.

Still, let's face it: sometimes being a highly sensitive person is a big pain in the butt. After all, this world is not made for us. It's generally loud, impatient, and overwhelming. It's full of tragedy, drama, and big emotions that tend to seep through our skin even when they aren't our own. On our best days, we may still feel exhausted. Our worst days can be so painful even the strongest of us want to give up.

I'm in a Facebook group for highly sensitive people. One day, someone asked this question: "If you could switch off your high sensitivity permanently, would you?" Most people said, "No way, never." But there were still a good number who answered "yes." And you know what? I don't blame them a bit.

Being an HSP is not for the faint of heart, is it? Sometimes we get so overwhelmed we only wish we could turn it off and get a break. Feeling everything so deeply can hurt. I've been there.

Three years ago, my family and I were building a new house. The stress from this situation falls under the "first world problems" category, for sure. But trust me, it was still pretty stressful when the framers put the roof on wrong, leaving the upstairs floor hanging down into our front porch.

Combine construction project stress with real estate craziness and a tiny rental home with toxic mold issues and well water that sometimes didn't work—not to mention constantly arguing with a builder who made up thousands in extra charges and tried to explain it all away with inexplicable scratches on notebook paper—*oh,* and long highway commutes. It was a complete overload. I felt like I was losing my mind. I couldn't get through the day without a nap. The slightest stress left me shaking and weak. Even worse, I felt *useless.*

Maybe none of it would have been a big deal for a hardier sort of human with better nervous system regulation (we'll talk later about what that is). But for me?

Being so overwhelmed had me making the stupidest mistakes. Like, I put diesel fuel in my Honda Odyssey, y'all. Another day I backed it into a fence. My husband was sweet about it, though. He laughed and said it seemed like I wanted a new vehicle, since I kept trying to kill mine.

It seems like a funny story in retrospect, but at the time, I was not laughing. My brain was fried from overstimulation (we'll also talk more later about what this is). I found I couldn't write anymore, or even organize myself to keep up with my usual tasks. It was like my mind was an empty shell of its former self.

I couldn't deal with the stress anymore. I was walking around in a fog, important things went through my brain like a sieve, and every time I got in the car I was terrified I would crash and kill us all. My rock-bottom moment was when I felt my family would be better off without me, and that is a scary thought to have. But didn't my family deserve a mom and wife who could handle things instead of flaking out?

It was my own mom who reminded me of my worth (thanks, Mom). She said that my family didn't need a mom who was a great general contractor or driver (although being safe is a plus). They needed someone who had empathy and noticed what was going on with them. Someone who knew what they needed to thrive, someone who made sure they were loved and cared for. They needed someone sensitive to serve as the family's emotional glue.

They needed me. And you know what? Someone needs you too.

Yes, life might be easier if you weren't highly sensitive, but you weren't born for easy. You were born for a purpose. Do you see that in yourself? If not, my hope is that this book helps you strike up that vision.

As you read on, you're going to gain a better understanding of what you are really made of and how you can use your unique gifts to make an impact. Besides that, you're going to learn why some things really are more difficult for us than for others (Hint: it's not because you're lazy or aren't trying hard enough!) and some tips on how to work through it—while being kind to yourself in the process.

What works for non-HSPs doesn't always work for us, so we'll brainstorm how to adjust and accommodate for our needs. We'll also talk about ways to cope with the anxiety, overwhelming empathy, and emotional intensity we often struggle with. And yes, we're going to talk plenty about dealing with people— the good, the bad, and the ugly.

Of course, not everything in this book will resonate with you. How could it? We may all be highly sensitive, but we each have different experiences and genetic makeup. There are as many different viewpoints as there are people on the planet.

If something doesn't jive with you, feel free to skip ahead (not that you need my permission). Or, read on and use it to start a dialogue with yourself or someone else. How do you see things differently? What is true for you? Sometimes, getting a new perspective not only helps us understand others better, but our own selves, as well.

Disclosure: I am not a psychologist, doctor, or any kind of medical professional. I am also not a professional comedian, but I do try a little too hard to be funny.

My only expertise is having lived as an HSP and empath for several decades. Sure, I've done plenty of reading and research, but when it comes down to it, that's all I've got. All I can do is share my own little bits of wisdom, sprinkled in with curated information from experts. You can do with them as you choose.

What I'd really love is for you to read this book and feel like you're sitting around with a good friend, drinking wine or coffee, and being like, *"Oh my word, me too! All this time, I thought I was the only one!"*

We'll intersperse those moments with ones where we laugh so hard we snort our drinks through our noses. Because let's face it, being highly sensitive can be lonely—which is kind of ironic, because sometimes we want nothing more than to escape from people. But I suppose there is nothing lonelier than being around a bunch of people who don't understand you.

There are few things so lovely in life as connecting with people who really *get* your experience. We may not completely understand everything about one another, of course, but hopefully this book is enough to give you that warm, comfortable feeling of knowing you most certainly are not alone.

So, grab your favorite hot mug of yumminess, relax, and take this time to recharge as you read along. You're worth it.

Chapter 2
Being A Highly Sensitive Human

"We have to dare to be ourselves, however frightening or strange that self may prove to be." --- May Sarton

Right now you might be wondering, is high sensitivity some kind of medical condition? Should I ask my doctor about it? Can the pharmaceutical industry make a drug for us and advertise it on TV with videos of happy, beautiful people dancing to sped-up warnings of rectal bleeding and sudden death?

My personal answers are no, probably not, and yikes. Once again, I want you to remember this: *there is nothing wrong with being highly sensitive.*

And I hate labels as much as anyone. We don't want to hex ourselves by internalizing an identity that doesn't serve us. That being said, internalizing the trait of high sensitivity should not lead to a negative view of oneself. This isn't a disability or a flaw. Being highly sensitive means your nervous system works very well! It makes you really good at a lot of things, which we'll discuss more as we go on. As an HSP, you truly have a bit of a superpower.

Of course, we also need the humility to recognize where we get hung up. Many situations are more difficult to navigate with an amped-up nervous system. Learning to work with what we have is essential to functioning at our best, and that's what this book is all about.

Highly sensitive people can always use some cheerleading, not to mention coaching. Heaven knows we've had our share of discouragement. It's time we turn the tables, find our inner strength, and own our gifts. Don't you agree?

As you learn more about yourself, don't be afraid to tell *your own story*. By being bold, we empower others to step out of the shadows too. And hey, the rest of the world isn't shy about blabbering on, so why should we stay quiet?

Perhaps you're still a little foggy on this whole "highly sensitive" thing. I'm sure many of you have already read Dr. Aron's book (or several of her books), but some likely have not. If you're in the latter group, put her on your reading list ASAP. But to satisfy your curiosity, let's quickly clear up what a highly sensitive person (HSP) is, and what it isn't.

But first, remember: I'm not here to tell you whether you are highly sensitive or not, or to what degree. Remember, this isn't about labels or any kind of diagnosis. It's about being your best self and laughing until your drink shoots out your nose. OK?

In *The Highly Sensitive Person*, you'll find the 2012 Author's Note sums it up nicely. There, Dr. Aron gives a description of the trait using the acronym "D-O-E-S."[1]

- *"D is for depth of processing."** This means our highly sensitive brains work harder than on average. They process every minute detail in our environment and subconsciously weave new information with our previous knowledge. Because of this, some of us tend to know things without knowing exactly how we know them. If you've experienced this, you know what I mean. Simply, it's intuition. We may need a little more time making decisions, but we usually choose well, showing a high level of both insight and foresight.

- *"O is for being easily overstimulated."** Because doing the above is exhausting! When there is too much information coming in, we get to the point where we just can't handle it anymore. This sometimes leads people to think something is wrong with us. They wonder why we seemingly can't deal with as much as others can. In reality, because of our depth of processing, we are handling *more* under the same circumstances. It's almost like we're missing a standard-issue filter on our nervous systems. Of course, this isn't always a bad thing. In a gentle environment, we do just fine. We just need more sleep and downtime, and we need to be more choosy about which situations we put ourselves in.

- *"E is for giving emphasis to our emotional reaction and having strong empathy, which among other things helps us notice and learn."** HSPs may be the first to be moved to tears, as well as the first to be quickly overcome with laughter when appropriate. (Drink snorting, anyone?) Admit it, once we get caught in the giggles, it's hard to stop! We also quickly react to the feelings of others, often without them needing to express anything verbally. News of violence, cruelty, unfairness, or injustice done to humans or animals cuts us to the core. We may even feel physical pain from another's experience as though it was partly our own.

- *"S is for being sensitive to all the subtleties around us."** Highly sensitive people notice what others miss. We observe the slightest shifts in an environment, often giving us the "feeling" something is off or about to happen. Some of us are very aware of (and perhaps irritated by) everyday smells, tastes, and sounds. We also pick up almost imperceptible changes in another person's demeanor, sometimes making it seem like we "read their mind" because we knew what they wanted or needed at the moment.

* Signifies quote from Dr. Aron. Descriptions are my own

interpretations.

So what do you think? Does "D-O-E-S" resonate with you? If you still aren't sure, you can go to Dr. Aron's website and take a self-test: https://hsperson.com/test/highly-sensitive-test/

You know what? It's OK if you're not sure, or if you don't feel super sensitive all the time. This is not an exclusive club, and there is no contest or prize going out for the most sensitive soul. We all just want to understand ourselves, and as a bonus, maybe even be understood by others. Whether the HSP label completely fits or not, you picked up this book for a reason, and I bet there is something in here just for you.

A lot of us have never felt like we fit in. Even among close friends and family, there was always that nagging feeling of "no one really understands me." When we find out there's a reason we feel different, and that there are others who feel the same, it's literally a game-changer.

Knowing you aren't alone gives you courage and strength. You need to know someone has your back, be it your community or a higher power.

The other place we find strength is inside ourselves. It's been there all along, even if yours seems to disappear just when you need it. Trust me, despite sometimes feeling like we've lost it, our strength is *still there*. Some of the most mentally strong, powerful, and resilient people I know are HSPs and empaths.

Part of accessing your inner strength is acknowledging who you are as an individual and what unique gifts you have to offer.

Too many of us have internalized a message of, "Who do you think you are? No one is so special." Besides that, our gifts probably didn't fit society's ideal of usefulness (we will talk more about this too). Therefore, we've picked up a truckload of limiting beliefs, hauling them around wherever we go. Perhaps we've even gotten used to hiding who we really are in order to fit in.

Well, my friend, it's time to dump that load of you-know-what. We're about to start peeling back the layers of what we've been told and figuring out what might actually be true instead. Next, we'll take a look at the pretty awesome gifts of sensitivity, and let you explore what kind of sensitive secret talents you've been blessed with.

Have you ever asked for a secret recipe, only to discover it just can't be recreated by anyone else? My husband has that magic touch with food. I can make something with the same ingredients, exactly how he told me to make it, but it just isn't the same as when he makes it himself.

You also have a unique "secret sauce" that no one else can copy. No one else can cook up an experience quite like the one you were made to live! We might imagine that famous people like J.K. Rowling or Meryl Streep are rocking their secret sauce. Maybe, but making the most of your gifts is not dependent on becoming famous or making gobs of money. It simply means you are being your authentic self and using your talents in a way that makes you happy and serves others. It doesn't matter how seemingly small of an impact you make, your contributions are needed and valuable.

After uncovering the special gifts we've been blessed with, we're going to do some transformative work. Here you'll see what might be holding you back. You'll be able to try out tools curated just for your highly sensitive self.

And don't worry, despite what poet and novelist May Sarton said at the beginning of this chapter, you probably won't find your sensitive self too frightening or strange.

By the time you're done with this book, my hope is for you to feel strong, resilient, and empowered to *own* your unique gifts.

---

1. ARON, ELAINE. "Author's Note." Highly Sensitive Person: How to Thrive When the World Overwhelms You, 25th Anniversary ed., Citadel Pr, S.l., NY, 2013.

Chapter 3

Elephants

"Can you remember who you were before the world told you who you should be?" --- Charles Bukowski

You know, I never really thought about having a favorite animal until I had kids. When you have little ones, you're constantly peppered with questions like, "What day will it be in 100 days?" "What would life be like if tacos were never invented?" and, "What's your favorite animal? Has it changed since last week?"

And by golly, you'd better come up with some answers. After many deep conversations with my minis, I realized my personal favorite animal is the elephant.

Elephants have such amazing personalities and emotional depth. They are gentle, empathetic, and never forget a friend. And yet, who can deny an elephant's strength?

Does anyone say, "Hey, Elephant, if you really want to be powerful, try being a lion. Don't you want to have the strength to hunt something down and kill it?"

Well, wouldn't that be a stupid thing to ask? The elephant doesn't have anything to prove. It's strong just the way it is.

We sensitive types are a lot like elephants. We aren't out looking for a fight, but if anyone crosses us, our family, or our values, they just might get a good stomping. Yet, we also may find ourselves preyed upon, taken advantage of due to our gentle nature. Some of us are even chained up by cultural ideals, not realizing we've had the strength to break out all along.

So let's talk a little about these cultural chains, shall we? We'll call them "limiting beliefs" for the sake of those with less flair for the dramatic. Whatever you call them, we all have them in some way, shape, or form.

Limiting beliefs are based on the stories we have picked up throughout our lives. They've shaped our views about who we are, how the world works, where we fit in, and what is possible for us. Our families, communities, and schools tell us these stories, and often act them out for us.

We've heard these stories so many times we assume they must be true, but when we stop and think about it, we often don't have any evidence for their truth—except for the sheer number of times these narratives have been repeated.

Some of these cultural narratives tell us what to do (go to college, get a good job, invest in a 401K, take the kids to Disney World). Others tell us *how to be* (gregarious, quick on the uptake, fearless, competitive, Type A, a real go-getter). And if we don't fit inside the boxes these stories create? Well, we may start to believe something is inherently wrong with us.

Why are we talking about cultural belief systems in a book about sensitivity and resilience?

Because as a highly sensitive person, you probably didn't fit in with modern cultural ideals (at least not all of them). Over time, feeling like you don't fit in often erodes self-esteem and gives us a wonky view of who we are and what we are capable of.

This isn't about blaming anyone for the way we are, but rather about learning that to uncover our true strength, we have to start chipping away at what holds us back.

There is something I want you to keep in mind as we go on: even though we each carry many stories passed onto us by family, culture, and society, the story now belongs to you. Right now, you get to choose what narratives you want to keep and which ones you want to lay aside.

For instance, when I mentioned a cultural ideal of the family that goes to Disney World, you might have thought, "Well, of course I want to take my kids to Disney! I love it more than they do!" Many highly sensitive people would be on that spinning teacup right along with you.

On the other hand, maybe the idea of a giant theme park filled with noise, smells, and long lines makes your head want to explode.

Personally, I'm in Camp Exploding Head.

Besides, my three kids all have varying levels of high sensitivity. Still, I always felt guilty about not taking my brood to The Happiest Place on Earth, even though I knew our sensitive nervous systems would make it a nightmare, because that was what society was telling me I should be doing. But you know what? It was the right choice for us.

I actually asked the kids last year if they wanted to go, and they responded with a resounding "Heck NO!" And I was like, "Boys, I need to get that response in writing. I don't want to hear any future whining about how your childhood was deprived of Mickey Mouse."

Even though this is a silly, non-life-changing example, the point is this: you don't have to do anything because "everyone else" says you should. What most people enjoy or what works for them may not work for you, because *you aren't like everyone else.*

So let's take a bird's eye view of some of the common cultural stories that might affect HSPs. As you read on, look at your own life experiences with curiosity. How have you been shaped by your environment? By others' expectations? What might be possible that you've always been told was impossible? What else might be true for you?

This is a lot bigger than a choice of theme parks, y'all. From here on out, you are writing your own story.

The Stories: Personality & Productivity

I'm sure you have heard someone not-so-humbly brag, "I'm just so Type A!", referring to the popular personality theory categorizing how different people respond to stress. Does anyone ever brag about being a Type B?

I grew up thinking Type B people were some sort of lazy, second-class citizens who maybe leaned toward psychosis. No one ever talks about "The B people," so I just assumed it wasn't good and you didn't want to be one of *them*.

Well, imagine my surprise upon finding out Type B personalities are laid back, creative people who strike a balance between their personal and professional lives. They lack the time-urgency and free-floating hostility possessed by Type As.

Um, hello? Is that a bad thing?

Honestly, I'm Type AB. I'm burdened by a Type A ambitious streak, which is ever-so-frustrating because I also have a Type B lack of time urgency. Sigh. Anyway, the point is, society has put Type A on a pedestal when Type B is every bit as valuable and needed. The result is a society that is in too much of a rush to slow down and show some compassion.

We have kindergarteners who can't stay home and rest when they have a cold. After all, they're nearly six. It's time for them to think about their future. We also see animals dumped at kill shelters because they take up too much time and make too much of a mess. And sadly, the elderly and disabled often don't get many visitors, because everyone is just so darn busy.

Of course, most Type A people don't like any of this either! We all wish it was different.

No matter what letter you identify with, we all want the freedom to do what is best for our loved ones—but when a society has been constructed without counsel and balance from the more sensitive Type Bs, we end up with a system designed for productivity at all costs. The needs of people are bowled over in a rush to get tasks completed. This leaves all personality types feeling a bit like cogs stuck in a machine.

Depending on your family of origin, you might have been schooled in "productivity at all costs" from the get-go. But even if you came from a more sensitive family, once you entered public school you likely learned quickly what was expected.

In the United States (where I live), our school systems were not designed to have much sensitivity toward children as individuals. The public school model was a product of the Industrial Revolution, and it was structured to create a compliant workforce who knew just enough to be useful. For those raising an eyebrow, this really is just history (the kind of history we didn't learn in school, ironically). If the subject interests you, check out *The Underground History of American Education*, by two-time New York State Teacher of the Year, John Taylor Gatto. I think you'll find it eye opening.

By the way, as we talk a little about the experience of an HSP in school, please don't think I'm being disparaging of the teaching profession. There are many wonderful teachers who are working their butts off and doing all in their power to serve the kids in their care. And I know they sometimes feel like cogs stuck in a machine too, wishing they had more freedom to meet the needs of each individual.

Unfortunately, many HSPs quickly find out the school system was not designed for us. The constant buzz of activity, no space to oneself, working in groups, bells ringing, noticing the emotions of the other children when no one else seems to, being put on the spot to answer questions, all the eyes staring at you, snotty-nosed kids reaching over and touching your food at lunch—school seems to contain a perfect storm of overstimulation.

Still, maybe you did quite well in school. Perhaps you even enjoyed some of the things I mentioned. Even if they are an A student or gifted athlete, a highly sensitive child often finds themselves turning inward in an effort to escape the things causing them to be overstimulated. Their teachers and classmates start to label them as quiet or shy, even though the child may be neither one in a more comfortable situation.

After a few years of this, the poor kid becomes painfully aware they do not meet the cultural ideal of the fun-loving, outgoing, go-getter personality. As much as they would love to have fun and express themselves enthusiastically, they just *can't*. The child doesn't understand what overstimulation is, but day in and day out, they are shut down by it.

Was that child you? It was definitely me.

Maybe your childhood school experience was totally different. After all, we each have different levels of sensitivity and unique biology. We all also receive varying levels of support from the adults in our lives. Whatever your story, you might find it interesting to think about how being highly sensitive affected your early life experiences. Here are some thoughts to mull over: Did you have a hard time keeping up with certain expectations? Were you sick and worn out much of the time? Perhaps you tended to freeze up when under pressure and ended up feeling stupid. Maybe you have a hard time "being yourself"? Did people label you with descriptions you later realized weren't true? And how about feeling like your worth was defined by how well you performed? Did you learn to attach your personal value to the grade at the top of your paper, or whether you won the game?

The more you identify as "Type A," the more likely it is that you've internalized the idea that your worth as a human is unbreakably tied to your level of productivity. I think this is the most insidious message, both because it permeates our culture so deeply and because it creates a kind of inner self-destruct button that is triggered whenever we can't keep up.

The belief that worthiness is measured by how much and how well we produce degrades the innate spiritual value of a human being. As highly sensitive people, we know we are more than flesh robots working on an assembly line until the day we break down. And yet, we feel the pressure as heavily as anyone.

Why are we talking about this again? (Let's make sure you're still with me.) As a highly sensitive person, you need to know *you are needed.* You have important work to do, work that makes a difference in people's lives.

And yet, that work may not always be viewed as "productive." It may not be the easiest to quantify, the most obvious to see, or the job commanding the highest monetary value.

Upon realizing this, you might have tucked your work away, viewing it as unimportant. Maybe, you reason, you'll pull it out later, once all the pressing matters of productivity are accomplished.

Except for that day never comes, does it?

Right now, you need to know this: what you have tucked away is highly valuable, and quite possibly a work only you can do. Yes, really. *You*, my friend, are irreplaceable. Remember that.

If you've struggled with feeling like you aren't enough, or can never do enough, you aren't alone. As I shared with you in the first chapter, I've wrestled with those feelings of worthlessness myself.

The things we sensitives excel at are often viewed as unnecessary. Taking care of people? That's sweet, but hurry up with it. Creating beauty? Cool, but only if it makes enough money. Thinking deeply? Overrated. Just regurgitate the information you've been given.

We all feel that pressure to hurry up, to be productive—oh, and don't forget to look good doing it.

When we struggle to meet those expectations, we deal with it in two ways, either:

A) Accept that we are "less than" and lower our expectations, or

B) Dig our heels in and work twice as hard, hoping no one will call us out on being unworthy.

Like I said, I've got that ambitious streak, so I picked Option B. And honestly, I wasn't very successful with working twice as hard. I just ended up burning out twice as fast. I actually thought I was quite resilient, though, because I always got up and tried again!

Hustle, crash, burn, repeat.

It turns out that I wasn't so much being "resilient" as "stubborn." We all know the definition of insanity: doing the same thing over and over again, but expecting a different result. That was me. Each time I thought, "This time, I'm going to follow through and stay disciplined!"

If you're wondering what I was trying to be more disciplined about, the answer is pretty much everything, usually all at once. I was constantly analyzing how I could do better and do more. Except eating sweets and carbs. Always trying to do that less, right? Schedule, produce, schedule, produce. Struggle to keep up appearances. Crash, burn, let it all go to pot. Try again. And again. And again.

I thought, maybe I just didn't have enough information—so began my dive into personal development books, podcasts, classes; maybe if I could just find the secret, I could finally get my act together.

One of the first personal development books I read was *Failing Forward* by leadership expert John Maxwell. It was a game changer for me. I've read and listened to a lot of his work since then, and I learned a lot about discipline and leadership because of it. I also loved listening to motivational legends like Brian Tracy and Jim Rohn.

But somewhere in the middle of an eight hour Audible recording telling me how to be a more successful human, I had a realization. Growing up, I lacked a good father figure (consider this as the understatement of the century). In my choice of reading material, I was basically curating my own patriarchy. I mean, a person could do worse than picking Zig Ziglar for fatherly advice, but take in too much of a good thing and you end up off balance.

Just like Type A ("get 'er done!") needs the balance of Type B ("let's think about this"), stereotypical patriarchal advice needs a dose of matriarchal wisdom to maintain an equilibrium.

Of course, this is a one-hundred percent cliche way of conveying it. We all know there are plenty of highly sensitive men and highly un-sensitive women, but the point is, viewpoints from all different personalities and energies are necessary and valuable.

For example, I was listening to one recording when I heard this quote by American businessman and author W. Clement Stone: *"If you cannot save money, the seeds of greatness are not in you."*

Darn, that is harsh! I mean, managing money is an important skill, but if you haven't figured it out yet, it just means you haven't figured it out yet. You probably weren't taught how, and you were likely handed down a crappy money mindset from your family. Seriously, you are not a loser just because you're still learning.

I am one-hundred percent sure that every human has their challenges, and that we can all benefit from sensitivity and understanding as we work through them.

So back to my mission of hustling to prove something to my imaginary patriarchy. All that pesky "Type AB" ambition had me spinning my wheels. I was getting nowhere except burnt out. Eventually, I started to wonder why I was putting myself through all this nonsense. Why do any of us try so hard to prove our worth through productivity, money making, or physical beauty?

I think it's because, deep down inside, we carry around a belief that if we are perfect and perfectly productive, we'll finally earn love, safety, and belonging. We will finally be enough, we will finally be OK.

The Type As and the Type Bs, the boy in school hoping to bring home an A to make his mom happy and the little (or not-so-little) girl with daddy issues—they all want the same thing, the most basic human desires: love, safety, belonging.

We crave acceptance from our tribe because throughout history, acceptance meant survival. And sometimes we go about it all wrong because we've been sold a lie: that we don't deserve to belong, that who we are isn't enough.

Yes, having a good work ethic is a wonderful thing. We need to be able to do good work and take care of our loved ones—my goodness, I am so grateful for my husband, who is the hardest working guy I know. But you know what? If he got sick and couldn't lift a finger, he would not be worth any less to me. I wouldn't love him any less. Don't you feel the same about your loved ones? I bet you do.

Humans are worth so much more than what can be quantified in terms of money, productivity, physical beauty, or traditional success. We know this is true, yet we struggle with feeling unable to ever do or be enough.

Most of us have been sold on the hustle. Starting early in life, a picture was painted for us of an ideal way to exist in the world and earn our keep. But when we reach out to grasp it, we come out empty handed. Turns out, it was all an illusion. There is no secret waiting outside of you, because you had what you needed all along.

Like our lovely elephant, you were never supposed to be a lion. The world has always craved your gentleness, empathy, and quiet strength. You have so much to offer. Who you are was always enough.

So, don't you think it's high time you ditched your limiting beliefs and broke out of those mental chains? Let's talk more about what is possible for you. Let's discuss the truth of what a highly sensitive person can really do.

Chapter 4

The Gifts of Sensitivity

"Musicians must make music, artists must paint, poets must write if they are ultimately to be at peace with themselves. What humans can be, they must be." --- Dr. Abraham Maslow, Psychologist and creator of Maslow's hierarchy of needs.

When you were a child, what did you want to be when you grew up? Did your life turn out as you planned? Maybe a fortunate few of us can say yes, but for most of us, adult life hasn't exactly fulfilled our childhood expectations.

I remember three of my early career goals. First: fashion designer. I spent countless hours designing my own catalogs, perfecting my custom line down to prices and color options. Unfortunately, when it came to actually making the clothing, I never got past learning to sew on buttons—though I still get heart eyes when I think about weaving textures and colors into perfection.

In my older years, I decided a career as a lawyer or psychologist would be more of a sure thing. Since highly sensitive people like me have a strong sense of justice, being drawn to the law was natural— and I was obsessed with Perry Mason, so there was that. As for my fascination with psychology, that likely came from being surrounded by crazy people.

Kidding!

(Kind of.)

Sometime when I was aspiring to become the female Carl Jung, my mom said something to me I'll never forget: "Jen, you'll never be happy unless you are doing your art."

The moment she said it, I knew she was 100 percent right. And yet, my next thought was, *"Yes, but does it matter?"*

Yup, even in my preteen years I had come to the pragmatic conclusion that being happy was not a priority. Be productive, make money, do something people will admire. That's what the world had taught me. Why should I expect to be happy? No adult is happy— or so it seemed, from my point of view.

But of course, my mom and Dr. Maslow (quoted at the beginning of the chapter) were correct: what humans can be, they must be. We can't abandon part of who we are and expect to be at peace with ourselves, for if we do, we'll always be a bit tortured by the nagging feeling that something is missing. It's like the thought that incessantly pokes at you when you forgot something important, because you *did* forget something important. *You forgot who you were supposed to be.*

As we considered in the last chapter, it's no wonder we get confused along the way. For most of our lives, we've been squeezed into a mold, one that probably wasn't well suited to our sensitive nature. Over time, we broke off more and more parts of ourselves that didn't fit into the mold and laid them aside. Is it any wonder we wind up feeling like something is missing?

In order to get our strength and confidence back, we have to retrace our steps, find what we lost, and take it back into our possession. In the last chapter, we did a little retracing and explored where we might have dropped some important pieces of ourselves. Once again, this isn't about, "Poor sensitive me, no one understood me and now I'm a mess." The point isn't to blame anyone for not understanding us in the past, but to understand *ourselves,* right now.

As we gain a better understanding of ourselves, something really strange tends to happen: we start to actually *like* ourselves. And maybe—gulp—we even begin to love and appreciate who we are. Crazy, right? And it feels pretty good.

But then, something even more curious transpires: our minds pull out a big ol' lasso and start roping us back into the Self-Doubt Corral.

You didn't even know your mind had a lasso, did you? But it's true, we all have one. Its job is to make sure we don't wander too far past our comfort zone, where our mind knows we'll be nice and safe. The lasso is doing its job when we find ourselves sabotaging our own progress, or having thoughts like, "Who do you think you are? You're not good enough to do this!"

Sound familiar? Well, hold on, cowboy. As we go through this chapter, we're going to be wrangling with some tough Who-Do-You-Think-You-Are lassos. I invite you to push through and really think about what special blend of sensitive genius you were blessed with.

You're probably going to have some resistance to this idea, like, "Me? Nope, I don't have any genius in me. Besides, wouldn't it be kind of braggy to admit if I did? Nobody likes someone who thinks they're so special."

It's true, bragging is ugly! But in acknowledging our gifts, we aren't tooting our own horn. I've said it before and I'll say it again: everyone has their secret sauce. But as you discover yours and others notice it, you may find things going something like this:

Friend: Ooh...what's that you got there?
You: Nothing.
Friend: Um, that doesn't look like "nothing." That looks like secret sauce.

You: Oh, that? No, really, it's nothing. I don't have any secret sauce.

Friend (Peering to get a better look.): Really? Are you sure? Because it looks a lot like secret sauce to me. And actually, it looks pretty good!

You (Blocking their view): No, no, it's just something I threw together. Not even close to being finished. Move along, nothing special to see here.

Friend: Well, okay. But if you're ever ready to share...

You: 'Kay, I'll keep you posted. Bye!

Now, isn't that silly? Why are you hiding your secret sauce? Everyone, highly sensitive or not, has something special to share. When people feel free to express who they really are and lean into their gifts, everyone benefits. Being your best self is, therefore, *not* an egotistical pursuit, as it allows you to serve others at your optimum capacity.

As you read on, remember this: *you have full permission to own your gifts*. You didn't get that permission from me; it's the inborn right of every human being. Every gift is special, but no gift is better than any other gift, so let go of the pull toward comparison. Humanity has a vast array of unique talents and perspectives, and all are needed. Don't waste your valuable energy hating on what you or anyone else has to be proud of, OK?

So let's dive in. We'll start by talking about the five most common types of sensitive people—the healer, the creator, the inventor, the visionary, and the sage—along with the unique gifts each of them carries. As you explore the sensitive types, you might realize you have a little of each, or you might realize you are *really* strong in one area. Others might feel their own unique type bubbling up separate from the five categories, which is entirely possible. After all, each of us has a unique, individual perspective, and we are each the world's only expert on our own lives. Just let this chapter be a starting point, a springboard to help you jump into the possibility of your own hidden potential.

Sensitive Type #1: The Healer

Have you ever had a stranger in a waiting room tell you their life story? Do you spend a good chunk of every party calming down a friend who's crying in the bathroom? If so, you just might hold the gifts of the sensitive healer.

The powers of healing are programmed into our bodies. Some of us are just particularly good at figuring out what people need to function optimally. Sometimes, what people need is just to be heard.

Usually, healing others by listening is perfectly OK with the healer, because they really hate small talk. Intuitively, they know their job is to sit with people through grief and breakdowns and to walk with them through transformation. They want to hear your stories so they know how they can help you heal. The healer doesn't know how to love you best if you won't talk about anything but the weather, or other people, or flat versus semi-gloss paint. Healers stare deep into your soul, kindly smile, and invite you to say just a little more.

People tend to open up to sensitive healers because they radiate warmth, comfort, and understanding. Whereas most feel uncomfortable with emotions and try to steer the conversation away from anything deep, the healer helps a person relax and spill their guts. They aren't just hearing what is coming out of someone's mouth; they are seeing and feeling the person's experience. The spoken word is almost secondary.

Unlike most, healers aren't eagerly waiting for a break in the conversation to interject their own story, or even thinking of what they are going to say next. The healer doesn't even realize to what extent they are tuning in to the other person's emotions because for them, it's just their normal way of listening. And honestly, it is very rare in this world for people to feel so deeply heard.

Of the three types, healers are the most in touch with the emotions of others, having a deep desire to protect and care for them. Their strength is truly in helping, serving, and forging strong connections with people and other living things. In this type, we find many of our empaths, who have a keen ability to sense the feelings and energy of others. (We'll go into the science of being an empath in the next chapter.)

In addition to providing emotional support, some sensitive healers have an intuitive understanding of what the body needs physically. They also usually understand that the emotional and physical can't be separated. This is especially true of healer moms, who are a force to be reckoned with. They will tirelessly dig until they become experts on nutrition and natural remedies, and they aren't afraid to explore complex topics like genetics and the immune system if it might help. Healers masterfully combine what they learn with intuition and empathy to care for their people. And of course, when professional care is needed, they won't stop searching until they find the best.

You might think our healers would become doctors, but often that is not the case. For an empath who almost feels another's pain in their own body, scalpels and blood aren't exactly a draw. Such a pity, isn't it? But don't worry, not all is lost—they can still heal us, outside of the operating room. With a health care system that breaks the whole person into multiple specialties, sometimes offering a suffering person little more than a barrage of testing, a diagnosis code, and a pill, having a sensitive healer on your side is invaluable.

If you are a healer, you have to be conscious of your weaknesses: emotional exhaustion, being taken advantage of, and being prone to martyrdom. Hang in there—we are going to address all of these issues in the next chapters. For now, know your abilities as a healer are valuable and needed!

Sensitive Type #2: The Creator

Most people live on the surface of life, their reality based on what's in front of them and their personal experiences—but the sensitive creator is astonishingly different! This type's inner life isn't bound by physical reality; instead, they look at everything through a lens of imagination. Their minds bring to life what wasn't there before.

Through literary fiction, paintings, sculpture, music, and so on, the sensitive creator's work gives us all a glimpse into a dream world.

Of course, anyone can learn the mechanics and techniques of an art form. You know this if you've gone to one of those studio classes where everyone comes out with a big canvas painting of wine bottles. Everyone has some creativity in them, but the sensitive creator has the pull to go much deeper. Instead of just copying a pattern, creators have the ability to go off the rails and come back with something breathtaking. They have a deep desire to express themselves authentically, communicate their own vision, and create things of enduring value.

Out of our three sensitive types, artistic creators are usually the most in touch with their *own* emotions. Creativity and emotion go together like bread and butter—you could have one without the other, but it wouldn't be nearly as good. This is probably why we have the cultural stereotype of the crazy and/or tortured artist. When we dive deep into our minds to create, we sometimes find buried memories or traumas that follow us back to the surface. It's true, sensitive creators can be prone to ruminating and intrusive thoughts, but this doesn't mean you're destined for misery. (We'll work on this in Chapter 7, Resilience & Reframing, I promise.)

If you feel pulled to be a creator but don't create, it may be because your innate ability has been tied up by fear. If we are functioning in a fight, flight, or freeze mode, creativity is shut down. Also if we are feeling the need to control our environment to stay safe, we won't be free to surrender to the creative process. (Don't worry, we will talk about how to work through all of this later in the book.)

Sensitive Type #3: The Inventor

Here we have another type of sensitive creator. While every bit as creative, this subtype may find themselves more drawn to logic and science than they are to emotions and art. The inventor has an intuitive understanding of how things work and uses their depth of processing to grasp complex ideas that go right over others' heads.

If you are this type of creator, you probably don't let many people see how amazing you really are. You're really a nice person but probably struggle to let people in. Well, I see you! And we need your brilliance as well as your kind heart.

Sensitive Type #4: The Visionary

So, how do you know if you're a visionary? Well, are you accustomed to people looking at you like you have two heads when you talk? Yes? Then, there you go. You're a visionary—and so am I!

Really, visionaries are big-picture thinkers who see things differently than most. If you fit this type, you might have episodes of clarity when you know something without knowing quite how you know it. It isn't any wonder people raise their eyebrows when the visionary speaks their truth. After all, it's this sensitive type's job to show others a new viewpoint.

Remember how the healer type detests small talk? Visionaries hate it too. There are so many fantastic thoughts swirling in their minds, it almost feels like torture to hold it all in and chat about the mundane.

No matter how much a visionary loves a cute pair of shoes (and believe me, personally I do), we crave deep discussions on things more important than leopard pumps. We feel called to share our vision—and yet it can be a lonely road as we navigate just how to do that.

There are three major characteristics of the visionary type: powerful intuition, a thirst for knowledge, and a strong sense of justice. Their deepest desire is to understand the laws of the universe and make life better for everyone.

The truth is, being a visionary is not for the faint of heart, and probably not a job most of us sensitives would pick. I mean sure, part of it is pretty sweet. You notice what others miss, seeing how seemingly unrelated things fit together. And you do it *almost* effortlessly, but not really, considering how much time you spend thinking and researching.

Your intuition isn't magic, nor is it infallible, but it does feel like a magic moment when all the puzzle pieces fall into place!

As much as we'd love the response of "Wow, thanks for helping me see that differently!" when we share our unique viewpoint, it doesn't always go down like that. It may be more like the scene from the end of *Invasion of the Body Snatchers* (1978 version), where Donald Sutherland's character points and screams as if to say, "*You're not one of us!*"

Sorry, visionary, it's true. You're different and it's hard to hide it.

The good news is you also radiate something special that people are drawn to. Your strong sense of justice leads you to be a voice of reason and a defender of the disadvantaged. As a visionary, you don't let anyone mess with your people. You're the picture of gentle strength, like the mama elephant protecting her baby.

Sensitive Type #5: The Sage

Maybe the visionary type sounds kind of like you, but not quite. The visionary is an idealist, maybe with a slight leaning toward rainbows and unicorns (Or maybe I'm just talking about myself. I do love unicorns), whereas you might be a bit more pragmatic. If so, you may be more of a sage.

The sage type has the clear-knowing of the visionary but also has the information and logic to back it up. Maybe you were born with a penchant for logic, or maybe you were just born into a thinker-type family where if you had a point to make, you'd better be able to prove it. Either way, you probably grew up as a bookworm and, over time, have gathered an impressive trove of knowledge. You've used your empathy and depth of processing to turn that knowledge into wisdom. Do you know how valuable your sensible judgment is in this crazy world? You, my friend, are priceless. Don't forget it.

Of course, being a visionary or sage isn't all rainbows, unicorns, and elephant snuggles. We often struggle with getting stuck in our heads, not taking action, and neglecting to take care of the physical or mundane aspects of life. And yes, we'll talk about ways to get past these issues as we go on.

So, which sensitive gifts have you been carrying around in your knapsack? Do you relate to the healer, creator, or visionary? Or perhaps the logic-driven creative inventor, or the sage? Maybe you have a mix of several types. I invite you to take a few moments to write down your thoughts.

If I totally missed the recipe for your secret sauce, go ahead and create your own type right now! There are a few questions in the journal to walk you through it.

Please, really do take some time to consider how much you have to offer. The gifts of sensitivity weren't given to you for no reason; they have a purpose. *You* have a purpose! I hope you will come out of this chapter with a fresh realization of how valuable and needed highly sensitive people are.

Still, we all have our struggles and may even feel very stuck. We need tools and healing to regain our strength before we can help anyone else, don't we? The next chapters are going to help you put on that oxygen mask and catch your breath.

Relax, breathe deep. Here we go.

Chapter 5

The Science of Being an Empath

"And now here is my secret, a very simple secret: It is only with the heart that one can see rightly; what is essential is invisible to the eye." --- *Antoine de Saint-Exupéry, The Little Prince*

Empaths have the beautiful ability to "see" with the heart. This makes us able to connect with other beings and our environment on a deep level. To some, this sounds kind of mysterious, and that's OK. We empaths can keep our secrets of seeing (and feeling) the invisible to ourselves if we like. Still, I do enjoy unraveling a good mystery, and that's what we'll do in this chapter as we explore the science of being an empath.

We've already talked about the work Dr. Aron has done to bring awareness to the trait of high sensitivity—particularly in the scientific community, where the phrase "sensory processing sensitivity" is more often used. Dr. Aron does mention having strong empathy as a characteristic of highly sensitive people, but being an empath takes the whole thing up a notch, well beyond the standard definition of high sensitivity.

Let's be honest: people can make being an empath seem pretty weird and woo-woo. This might lead to throwing out the whole concept of high sensitivity like a baby with the bathwater, which would be a pity. Being an empath isn't supernatural. Empathy, of course, is a very natural human ability; empaths just have it turned up more than average. In this chapter, we're going to break it down in a way that's understandable, logical, and totally un-woo-woo.

Although empaths have always existed, the concept of people who easily tune into and absorb the emotions of others is just starting to gain some traction. Honestly, until I read about it a few years ago, I was rather clueless about my own emotional sponginess. I didn't know why I was affected so profoundly by other people. Learning about empaths was a game-changer for me. When we understand why we are the way we are, it can be pivotal for our own development.

Still, the world hasn't quite caught up. I recently saw a post where a psychology student stated they hadn't found any scientific data proving empaths exist. Well, for a minute there I felt like a real live unicorn, sitting there, *existing*.

It's true, we empaths are real flesh and blood creatures. And believe it or not, we really can understand our mysterious selves—whether anyone else does or not!

Plus, there is scientific evidence to explain empathic ability. We'll get to that in a sec, but first, what exactly is an empath? Let's list some of their traits:

- Empaths are highly sensitive people who are very tuned in to the emotions of others—this goes beyond just noticing whether someone is in a good or bad mood. An empath actually feels the other person's feelings in their own body. For some, this includes feeling physical pain, to the point that it can be quite debilitating.

- As an empath, you sense the "vibe" of a room upon walking in. Similarly, you know when there is something off with the energy of an individual person. You may not always be able to put your finger on it, but you have a sense when someone is lying or hiding something. This can also extend to places or objects that give you the creeps.

- When you hear a tragic or emotionally intense story, you have a strong reaction—almost as though you were going through the experience yourself. You may have a hard time shaking it off and feel almost silly for being so traumatized by the story of a person you have never met. *(Psst...you are not silly at all!)*

- Your intense sense of connection likely also includes animals, and you feel fiercely protective of them. Empaths often feel a deep connection to nature and the earth, intuitively understanding how to care for things like plants. (Personally, I'm not a plant empath, although with practice I'm getting better at keeping them alive.)

- If you're an empath, you have a beautiful ability to understand people. Even if they are fumbling around with verbal expression, you *get* them and have an intuitive understanding of where they are coming from. Isn't it true we all crave being understood so clearly by another human being? Empaths really are wonderful to have around.

I bet you are curious as to how empaths got this way. Is there really a scientific explanation? Perhaps they have hidden antennae? No antennae (sorry to disappoint), but we do have something even cooler: *mirror neurons*.

Actually, everyone has them. Mirror neurons are a type of brain cell that is activated when we either perform an action or watch someone else performing the same action. From the time we are born, these cells enable us to learn through imitation. They also help us understand the actions, intentions, and emotions of other people.

Neuroscientist Marco Iacoboni explained it succinctly in an interview with Scientific American titled *The Mirror Neuron Revolution: Explaining What Makes Humans Social*:

> The way mirror neurons likely let us understand others is by providing some kind of inner imitation of the actions of other people, which in turn leads us to "simulate" the intentions and emotions associated with those actions. When I see you smiling, my mirror neurons for smiling fire up, too, initiating a cascade of neural activity that evokes the feeling we typically associate with a smile. I don't need to make any inference on what you are feeling, I experience immediately and effortlessly (in a milder form, of course) what you are experiencing. [1]

Aren't our brains fascinating? Humans truly are designed for connection. And while we all have mirror neurons and the ability to empathize, there are actually two types of empathy. There is cognitive empathy which involves *perceiving* what another person is thinking and feeling. And there is emotional empathy which means *feeling* what another person is feeling.

A psychopath can actually have strong cognitive empathy. In other words, they are good at reading people, which can make them dangerous manipulators if they choose to go down that road. On the other hand, empaths not only have the ability to read people, we also have strong emotional empathy. Emotional empathy has a bonding effect. A true empath would never take advantage of another being, because to hurt someone is not only unconscionable, but it hurts us too. Having both cognitive and emotional empathy, we not only tune in to others and understand, but we connect and care.

Many psychologists think this tuning in to others is related to how we interact with our caregivers when we are very young. For instance, if your parents were emotionally erratic or physically unreliable, you learned to pay closer attention to shifts in their behavior in hopes of getting your needs met. Perhaps you adjusted your own behavior in an effort to either get their attention or keep them calm. This early focus on others' emotions for survival may have resulted in you becoming an empath.

This can also happen with children who have medical issues leading to an interruption in their normal care. Personally, I was a NICU baby and had little personal interaction for that first part of my life, which makes me wonder if my brain started working hard at observing people right away. In reality, we may never really know what made us exactly how we are, but we do exist, and there is nothing wrong with us.

By the way, some empaths have an even more intense condition which may be linked to mirror neurons: *mirror synesthesia.* Synesthesia is a phenomenon in which one type of stimulation evokes the sensation of another. There are many different types of synesthesia. For instance, when a person hears a certain sound, they may involuntarily visualize a color. Mirror-touch synesthesia is when someone feels like they are personally being touched (or hurt) when they witness it happening to someone else.

People with synesthesia often don't tell others about their experience, no doubt because it's not fun to have people stare blankly at you like a deer in the headlights. If you happen to possess these gifts, know you aren't alone and once again there is nothing wrong with you. Your brain is just wired differently, and you are amazing!

Another scientific reason why empaths are so connected to and affected by others is electromagnetic energy. Did you know the brain and heart generate measurable electromagnetic fields? It's true. This is how commonly used medical technologies like electrocardiogram (ECG) and electroencephalogram (EEG) work.

Rollin McCraty, Ph.D., Director of Research at The HeartMath Research Center, published fascinating findings on this subject in his paper, *The Energetic Heart: Bioelectromagnetic Communication Within and Between People.* If you enjoy science, I suggest reading the whole thing. For now, here are a couple of quotes from the paper:

> Evidence now supports the perspective that a subtle yet influential electromagnetic or "energetic" communication system operates just below our conscious level of awareness. The results of these experiments have led us to conclude that the nervous system acts as an antenna, which is tuned to and responds to the magnetic fields produced by the hearts of other individuals. My colleagues and I call this energetic information *cardioelectromagnetic communication* and believe it to be an innate ability that heightens the awareness and mediates important aspects of true empathy and sensitivity to others. Furthermore, we have observed this energetic communication ability can be enhanced, resulting in a much deeper level of non-verbal communication, understanding, and connection between people. [2]

    Dr. McCraty found the heart's electromagnetic energy is not only transmitted internally, but was also detectable several feet away from the body with Superconducting Quantum Interference Device (SQUID)-based magnetometers. (It's OK if you just pictured an actual squid. I did too.) He also noted that patterns in heart rate variability were "distinctly altered when different emotions are experienced" and are "felt by every cell in the body". And his team showed data indicating "cells studied *in vitro* are also responsive to the heart's bioelectromagnetic field."
    Isn't that amazing? Our heart rate literally changes with our emotions, sending detectable energy out of our bodies! Yes, there is evidence showing our hearts can communicate without words.
    So, isn't it possible that some highly sensitive people are aware of the subtle differences in electromagnetic energy and are adept at "reading" the emotions of others? Scientific evidence put aside,

when you know, you know. The average person is generally aware of what it means to say "you could cut the tension in the air with a knife" or "I get a bad vibe from her". It's energy, and we empaths feel it more than anyone else.

I hope you have a better understanding of empaths and why we are the way we are. By way of review: Antennae? Not exactly. Mirror neurons, the heart, and electromagnetic energy? Yes. Glitter and unicorns? Maybe sometimes.

It sounds pretty cool, doesn't it? Well, it is, but at the same time, being an empath—like being highly sensitive in general—can be exhausting and stressful. Absorbing other people's negative emotions is often painful and confusing. If we don't heal our own past emotional wounds and properly equip ourselves to deal with our empathy, it can paralyze us. We might find ourselves stuck in unhealthy relationships or just hiding from people in general. If you're a struggling empath, I think the rest of this book is going to be very helpful to you.

Let's talk about two struggles specific to empaths: mirroring and sponging.

The Mirror

As an empath, do you ever feel like people don't see you? Do you find it really difficult to convey your own thoughts and feelings when another person is in front of you? Perhaps at times, you've had something you felt very strongly about, a clear message you wanted to convey, but you found as soon as other people started to talk, your own thoughts got blurry and hard to reach.

Afterward, you realized you hadn't said what you wanted to say. In fact, you were only able to get out what the other person wanted to hear, and you probably felt awful because of it.

One place I experienced this was the unfortunate time when I tried doing sales presentations. Even though I really loved the product I was selling, once I was face to face with a person, I couldn't convey my enthusiasm. Although people seemed to enjoy talking to me, and would often tell me their life stories in the process, I rarely got a sale. Eventually I realized that instead of expressing my feelings about the product, I was tuning in and reflecting back to the other person their own reservation to buy. In other words, I was mirroring them. Not exactly a winning marketing strategy.

Mirroring can happen in any situation where an empath either needs to convey a message, express a need, or resolve a conflict. When we pull out the mirror, other people don't see us and we don't get what we want or need.

What's wrong with me?! You might have thought after an interaction involving the mirror. *I feel so strong-willed, so why do I become so weak when I'm around others?*

Most of us really dislike this part of being an empath. We don't want to lose ourselves in other people; we want to communicate authentically and be seen for who we really are. Sure, sometimes people like us because we have an easy time joining them on their wavelength, but it can also feel yucky interacting with people this way. We often realize too late we're being a chameleon, and then we begin worrying people will think we're fake or weak-willed. The worst part? We aren't even doing it on purpose!

The truth is, you aren't weak. You're unconsciously being a mirror, which was a survival skill you developed a long time ago. Maybe it's those darn mirror neurons on steroids, causing us to lose ourselves in other people. Whatever the reason, it happens to many of us.

My personal opinion is that mirroring can be a useful tool for the healer. After all, mirroring allows us to tune in very deeply to another person's experience and understand them well. However, we must keep in mind that mirroring doesn't always serve us. We need to learn to use mirroring when it's helpful and break free of it when it's not.

If you tend to mirror others and lose yourself in the process, you may have picked up the belief that your needs, opinions, or ideas are not very important, or you might have learned to be hyper-tuned-in to others in an attempt to stabilize their moods and keep chaos at bay. Sometimes, we get so used to tuning in, we forget how to tune out.

If, in the past, we used mirroring as a way to stay safe (for example, in a chaotic home environment) and, throughout our lives, we've never quite shaken the feeling of not being safe, we might find we're always tiptoeing around other people. We can be subconsciously afraid of what might happen if we were to relax and be ourselves.

Holding that mirror can feel very comfortable because, after all, we are hiding behind it. The longer we've done this, the more we are used to not being seen. While hiding can give us a sense of comfort and protection, in the long term, it doesn't feel good. Plus, it makes it almost impossible to share your gifts of sensitivity when no one is seeing the real you. Even as a healer, you have to be seen and able to connect meaningfully with others.

At first, you don't have to force yourself to put down the mirror. Just notice. Start to recognize how it feels and at what point you start to slide out of yourself.

After a while, you will probably start to notice the moment where you let yourself slip away and tune completely into the person in front of you. After paying attention to these moments for a while, you'll soon be conscious of it enough to make a decision to back up and "stay in your own lane" [3] (to borrow a term from author and psychotherapist Dr. Terri Cole).

And what about before you're even in the situation? Let's say you have something important to present to a person or a group of people, perhaps an idea you feel very strongly about. But you know that darn mirror is going to stop them from even seeing you. Along with practicing what you're going to say, try practicing how you're going to *be*.

Do a little acting to see how it feels to show up with purpose. If you don't think you have it in you, is there someone you admire for their charisma and confidence? How would they show up to this challenge? There is nothing wrong with creating a little alter ego to carry you through situations where you might otherwise disappear. If you're worried this makes you a fake, consider the irony: your other option is acting like someone else altogether, against your will. I don't know about you, but to me, the alter ego doesn't sound half bad when compared with the mirror!

Remember: when you feel yourself starting to slip into mirroring, back it up and hold on tight! Your ideas are important, and you need to find a way to convey them! Do something physically grounding like wiggling your toes and pressing your feet into the floor. Notice your breath. This will help pull you back into being present in your own body.

Of course, sometimes it will be appropriate to go ahead, tune in, and let your empathy do its thing. It just needs to be up to you whether you want to use it or not. Once you're not using it all the time, you'll be less exhausted and better able to tune in effectively when you want to.

Now, when you do use your empathy, you need to learn how to protect yourself from negative energy and burnout. This brings us to our next topic:

The Sponge

Have you ever been minding your own business, happy as a lark, when someone walked in the room and their negative energy hit you like a ton of bricks? For some of us empaths, this can literally be physically painful. Sometimes we are overcome by someone else's emotions without even realizing where it is coming from.

Sponging may sound similar to mirroring, but there are differences. With the mirror, we act differently, reflecting back the other person's mood or personality. It actually feels pretty good in the moment because we feel safe and avoid conflict. Whereas sponging involves taking on other's emotions, pain, or negative vibes. It may not change how we act, but it changes how we feel. Sponging can happen even without having much interaction with the other person, and it can really wear an empath out.

Non-empaths wonder why everything is so exhausting for us. They don't understand why we dread parties and crowded places. Well, this is why. We never know what energy we are going to get hit with. Even a positive, happy atmosphere can be overwhelming, because empaths often are in the habit of constantly scanning the room to make sure everyone is OK and nothing is unsafe. How draining! It's no wonder we often can't wait to be back in the comfort of our own homes.

Of course, some empaths are extroverts and can handle a lot more people-ing and partying than introverts. My son is like this, and so is one of my good friends. They love being with people and doing all the things—but afterward, even they are going to want some downtime to decompress.

Extroverted empaths get energy from positive interactions and joyful occasions, but when there's negativity involved, they find it mentally and physically draining. They are probably the ones who coined the phrase, "People: can't live with 'em, can't live without 'em." Meanwhile, introverted empaths are usually like, "Eh, I think I could live without 'em." (Joking. Kind of.)

Surely, both extroverted and introverted empaths love their favorite people, but it's often a struggle. We like to think being empathetic makes us nice people, and we usually are, but without proper emotional boundaries, we can end up behaving toward others in unhealthy ways.

After all, sponging up the emotions around us gets quite tiresome. When you're in a great mood and suddenly soak up someone else's bad vibes, it's pretty darn irritating, right? We might start to think, "How dare you come in with that dark cloud over your head and mess up my day?"

As much as I hate to admit it, sometimes getting all mixed up in other people's feelings makes us empaths act a bit selfishly. We think, *Can't they just hurry up and be done with these feelings? It's really messing with me!* We may forget about the fact that the other person has every right to feel those feelings for as long as they need to.

We can even become a little manipulative because we're so desperate for people to respond in a way that doesn't set off our empath sirens. It's easy to fall into a pattern of trying to control others' reactions so we don't have to absorb negativity.

I love this quote from author Seth Godin: *"Empathy can simply be a willingness to let people be who they want to be and not insist that they be who you want them to be."*

Soak *that* up for a moment, my spongey friends.

Because empaths tend to feel others' pain we have to practice purposeful detachment. Of course, we are going to notice the experience of the other person and empathize, but then we have to be willing to step back and let them own their own experience. So how do we do that exactly? As is the case with mirroring, the first step is just *noticing*. What are you feeling? Where is it coming from?

Since most of us are very visual creatures, it is sometimes helpful to visualize feelings, negativity, or electromagnetic energy as something we can see. For instance, you could picture another person's negative energy as a little glowing ball. Imagine you find it and pick it up. Once you realize what it is and who it belongs to, imagine handing it back to them. You might feel yourself smiling and saying, "Oh, this is yours. You can have it back." You detach from it, and step away.

"Finders keepers" is not a winning strategy for empaths. We have to let people keep what is theirs. The closer you are to someone, the more difficult it is—believe me, I get it. When someone in my family is upset, I feel it as physical pain. I have to remind myself over and over again that it's OK for them to be upset. They are allowed to be sad, angry, or disappointed, and I have no business rushing them through it. I can still be safe and OK, even if people around me aren't happy.

That is a very hard lesson for those of us who honed our empathic skills during trauma to learn. If you find yourself acting in unhealthy ways because you feel unsafe around other people's strong negative emotions, it might be helpful for you to find a therapist who specializes in trauma. Sometimes we have to sweep out some old memories to make room for new ways of doing things, and therapists have tools to help you in the process. There's no need to go it alone.

I did some of this work when I was going through my training in Aroma Freedom Technique. It's vital for those of us who are drawn to healing professions to learn how to do our work without sponging up negative energy. My teacher, Dr. Benjamin Perkus, walked us through an Aroma Freedom Technique session specifically focused on the tendency to soak up others' emotions, which was incredibly helpful.

First, we processed through some of our own memories that were telling us to be hypervigilant of the emotions of others. After processing through these memories, I found myself more able to practice loving detachment. I could sit with someone as they processed their own emotions without soaking them up myself.

It's true, the deep work of processing emotional baggage is transformational—but I know you need tools you can use on your own, right now. So here's a little something for your empath toolbox: the Zipping Up visualization. I learned this from a fellow Aroma Freedom Technique practitioner who learned it from someone else, so I'm not sure where it originated. Kudos to the smart people who come up with this stuff.

To begin, as with any visualization exercise, start by noticing your breathing. Get really present in your body, feeling your feet on the floor and your bottom in your chair as you sit.

Now, picture zipping yourself up in a warm, comfortable, protective suit. Visualize putting on the suit and, if possible, take your hands and sweep them up your body from your feet, all the way up over your shoulders, pulling up the cozy hood and tucking it around your chin. Zip it up snugly. Your suit radiates warmth; anything cold and negative just bounces right off. Take a few minutes to let this cozy, protected feeling sink into your body.

What does this visualization do? It simply calms your nervous system and helps you be present in your own body. Doing this exercise before being around a lot of people can create feelings of warmth and protection that will put you in a good space to handle the situation.

If you're an empath, you have a very special gift. I hope this chapter has helped you understand empaths a little better, and perhaps given you some ideas for coping with this special type of high sensitivity.

Unlike many people, most empaths don't fear emotions. Sure, sometimes we fear other people's emotional instability because of past trauma. But in general, we are very comfortable sitting with others who are grieving or need to emote. Because of this, we are typically better equipped to do the often difficult and uncomfortable work of helping others heal.

No one heals by burying the past, but that's exactly what most people prefer to do. They pretend it never happened, medicate, numb out, and avoid feeling as much as possible. But not us. That's why empaths are often in the business of breaking generational trauma and unhealthy patterns of being. Anyone has the power to say, "This stops with me." Highly sensitive empaths are often the ones who have what it takes to dig deep and finish the job.

Of course, being an empath isn't easy! That's why you're reading this book, after all, to build up the strength you need to do your work and thrive in a tough world. We've discussed how to deal with other people, but sometimes, *we* are the ones tearing our own selves down, from the inside. Why do we do this, and how can we stop? That's what we'll talk about next.

---

1. Iacoboni, Marco. "The Mirror Neuron Revolution: Explaining What Makes Humans Social." Scientific American, Scientific American, 1 July 2008, https://www.scientificamerican.com/article/themirror- neuron-revolut/.
2. McCraty, Rollin. "The Energetic Heart: Biolectromagnetic Interactions Within and Between People." The Neuropsychotherapist. 6. 22-43. 10.12744/tnpt(6)022-043.
3. Terri Cole. "Videos." Terri Cole, 11 Jan. 2020, https://www.terricole.com/videos/.

Chapter 6

Inside the Highly Sensitive Mind

"You're mad, bonkers, completely off your head. But I'll tell you a secret. All the best people are." --- Lewis Carroll, Alice in Wonderland

Highly sensitive people aren't usually the loudest in the bunch. Since we often need to process things deeply before we react or speak, some may assume we've got nothing to say. Maybe we even seem boring, to people who don't really know us.

Well, they have no idea what is going on under the surface! As theoretical physicist Steven Hawking said, "Quiet people have the loudest minds." Our sometimes well-guarded inner lives are rich and complex. Wouldn't you agree?

As a child, you may have had a vivid imagination, with worlds and playmates existing only in your mind—and maybe, like me, you resented when adults requested your presence in reality.

I recently had a conversation with my husband about kids paying attention when adults are lecturing (in school or otherwise). I said, "I never paid attention when I was that age. Did you?"

To my surprise, he was pretty incredulous. "Of course I paid attention," he said. "What were *you* paying attention to?"

Well my goodness, I never needed anything to pay attention to; my own mind could keep me entertained for hours on end. I had imaginary families who I designed entire houses for, down to the color of the hangers in their closets. Back then, I always had a storyline bubbling in my head and I wanted nothing more than to get home to my paper, pencils, and quiet so I could spill it all out.

Honestly, my old brain still keeps me quite entertained. The inner world of a highly sensitive person is a fascinating place, if I do say so myself.

Of course, it isn't all sunshine and rainbows inside our little heads, is it? As we grow up, we usually stop imagining what our stuffed animals are doing today and our dreaming becomes more realistic. Sometimes these dreams are positive—we imagine things we want to do and think about what is possible for us. Dreaming up ideas and making plans can be a wonderful catalyst for change and growth...but that isn't always the way it goes.

As we play things out in our minds, some dark clouds can start to form in our imaginary world. We wonder things like: what will people think? How will they respond to me? What if something terrible happens? Using that fantastic imagination, it's easy to come up with literally every worst-case scenario. Gruesome accidents. Ways of dying straight out of an episode of *CSI*.

And sometimes, just as bad, we torture ourselves by going over past scenarios, wrestling with regrets, and dreaming of how good life would be if only we'd done things differently.

So does it really matter what's going on in our minds? As highly sensitive and emotional beings, can we even control it? And do we even want to?

These are the questions we're going to chew on in this chapter.

The Power of Thoughts

Some might shrug it all off, assuming, "Oh well, it's only thoughts!" But the truth is, our thoughts aren't just fluffy little bubbles of nothingness. Thoughts produce chemical reactions in the body.

Neuroscientist, pharmacologist, and discoverer of the opiate receptor Dr. Candace Pert referred to these chemicals, or peptides, as *"the molecules of emotion"*.[1]

By envisioning our own untimely demise or ruminating on how much people dislike us, we can unwittingly trigger a chemical cascade to be released within us. These chemicals cause us to experience sensations we know as emotions.

Thoughts and emotions are real, and if we aren't careful, they can end up tearing us down from the inside out.

In the last chapter, we learned that electromagnetic fields generated by the heart permeate every cell in the body. Rhythmic patterns in heart rate variability are altered when different emotions are experienced. That means your thoughts and subsequent emotions are actually changing the way your heart functions, which is therefore affecting every cell in your body.

And we can feel that, can't we? We're physically aware of our emotions in our gut, our lungs, our muscles. Dr. Pert famously said, *"The body is your subconscious mind"*. There is no separating our thoughts from our bodies. Everything works together.

When we consider all of this, it's easy to see the true power of our thoughts. Our thoughts create chain reactions affecting our health, relationships, and ability to fully tap into our gifts of sensitivity. Our thoughts can sabotage the full and meaningful life we want to live.

When our minds are left to wander willy-nilly, it's like being in a tiny boat, tossed about on a rough sea. When a wave comes, you go with it, hoping that eventually things will calm down enough for you to relax, make some forward progress, and enjoy life. But that calm rarely sticks around for long, does it? And since highly sensitive people feel and process things more deeply, we can be in for one heck of a ride.

Obviously, it would be to our benefit to get a handle on what's going on between our ears—but actually doing that is another ball of wax.

You've likely heard the idea that you can't control everything, but you can control your reaction. We know this is true, but sometimes it's more complicated than it sounds.

To Control or Not to Control, That is the Question

When presented with the idea of reigning in one's thoughts, many people—even those who know it will be a challenge to change our way of thinking—are all in. Let's face it: thoughts lead to emotions, and emotions can hurt. It's only logical that we want to avoid pain.

Besides, riding the waves of our own emotions is exhausting enough, never mind being tossed about by the tumultuous waves of other people's emotions. We don't feel strong enough to take it anymore and will do just about anything to feel solid ground beneath us again.

Even if you aren't sure where to start, you likely realize it's possible to change how you think. And yet, we sometimes have resistance. Maybe it's being too overwhelmed with life to do the hard work of change, which is totally understandable, but I think it often goes deeper than that.

After all, as highly sensitive people, a number of us have it in our nature to place a high value on feelings. If this is you, emotions are a highly important factor as you make decisions. You also have a strong need to express yourself authentically, and to dismiss or manage your emotions probably seems very wrong and icky. And well it might!

Also, your emotional experience may feel like an integral part of who you are as a person. If you try to control or change your feelings, will you be able to stay true to yourself? Will you really be fixing anything, or will you just suppress your true experience? These are very legitimate questions.

Your emotions are real, and they have a purpose: to tell you something. Taking charge of your thoughts and emotions should not mean ignoring or blithely dismissing them. The point is to let them do their job, and then release them once they have served their purpose.

If you feel like changing your emotional experience would make you less *you,* consider that our thoughts are not always *our own* in the first place. Often, we've adopted an inner dialogue from our family of origin or someone else who had an influence on us. The words and the emotions that follow our inner dialogue could have nothing to do with who we really are as human beings! By repeating them, we're just going through learned patterns, often to our detriment.

Highly sensitive, empathic people are all the more prone to absorbing and internalizing the words and energies of those close to us. After all, we feel subtle shifts in people's moods and hear changes in tone others miss. A snide remark that bounced off someone else may have hit you right at your core, and especially as a child, those painful responses can get stuck in our minds and bodies, only to come out later in the form of our thoughts.

Someone once told me that whenever they make a mistake, they hear the words, "You never do anything right!" Well, obviously that isn't true. They do many things right. So where was this negativity coming from? This person realized the voice they were hearing belonged to their father, who had died many decades earlier. This person was a grandparent, but still had their dad's emotionally charged (but very wrong) message echoing in their thoughts, causing them pain.

Many of us have similar unchecked thoughts bouncing around in our heads. Freeing yourself from carrying around this kind of mental baggage allows you to finally become *more* authentically yourself, not less!

Sometimes we have to stop and ask, "Whose words am I repeating?"

OK, so not repeating negative messages from the past is one thing. But what about those persistent problems that tear us down from day to day? Are we supposed to ignore them and our feelings around them?

Good question. Here's another good question:

But Did You Die?

I don't think we can talk about changing our thoughts without first addressing toxic positivity. Positive thinking can create change, yet it's easy to swing the pendulum a little too far. It's all too easy to get addicted to not feeling the hard things.

We know how painful it was to be on an emotional roller coaster, and once we get off we usually don't ever want to go back. So when unpleasant feelings inevitably come up, we fear losing control. We are too quick to mentally flip the situation on its head without letting ourselves fully process what's happening.

We may feel like we're caught in the waves, frantically paddling back to shore, telling ourselves, "It could be worse! No one died! Everything happens for a reason! It's fine! Sunshine and rainbows. Sunshine and rainbows. Darnit, I am not losing control. I never want to feel those emotions dragging me down to the bottom again."

After a long time living this way, I eventually realized I wasn't "brave" as much as "terrified of losing control." I just wanted to avoid pain and had found a way to hide from it at all costs.

When we have anxiety and/or past trauma attached to the pain of feelings, we can easily end up pathologically avoiding painful emotions. This, my friends, is toxic positivity.

We can do this both to ourselves and to others, whenever we refuse to stop to allow for feelings. As highly empathetic people, we usually don't do this to others, but it happens.

Toxic positivity says, "It could always be worse! You have no business feeling bad! After all, you could be dead!" The truth is, your feelings matter, and they count. Life is not a contest to see who has it the worst, with only the winner allowed to feel something about it!

Once, I was sharing a little tidbit about my childhood with someone—not in a "feeling sorry for myself" way, just literally telling the story. The person I was talking to cut me off with a curt, "You didn't have it that bad."

I was shocked. I wasn't trying to express the situation's level of badness; I was just plainly saying what had happened—with maybe even a little humor interjected. Anyway, I personally know what it's like to have your story dismissed as unimportant because it "could have been worse."

Your story really is important, and your emotions are valid. It's vital that we are able to tell our stories without being judged as overly emotional or dramatic. Sometimes people will do this to you because they can't handle the emotions it brings up *for them*. Try not to shut down the emotions of yourself or others. Just because you didn't die doesn't mean it doesn't matter. It's your story, and your experiences and all the emotions you felt along with it are real.

Sure, we'd love to be happy all the time, but we can't just bury emotions under a pile of sunshine, rainbows, and unicorn poop. Remember, emotions are actually molecules that are physically affecting your entire body. If we bury them, they never die.

After years of running from and burying my feelings, I can finally see that true strength lies in the ability to sit with emotions and truly feel what they are trying to tell us. We are courageous when we resist the desire to flee and instead step into the emotion, feel it in our body, and accept its message. Really, the molecules of emotion are messengers of change. They are our friends, guiding us toward good and away from harm.

The reality of life is that we sometimes experience emotions like grief. These times are going to hurt, and no amount of positive thinking can make it go away. Sometimes we do the work to process our emotions and they still keep coming back. There are even some losses we will always grieve, as long as we live in this world.

Life and emotions are messy, and there is no neat, simple, logical formula for balancing feeling your emotions while keeping them in check. Perhaps, (much to the chagrin of my control-freak self), *control* is the wrong word when it comes to thoughts and emotions.

Sure, self-discipline has a role as we learn new ways of thinking and being, but what we really need is to make friends with our thoughts and emotions. We need to learn how to lovingly train our thoughts to serve us better. We also must respect our emotions and their messages, along with learning how to release them and move forward as needed. In the next chapter, I'm going to give you some "actually useful tips" for putting all of this mumbo jumbo together.

Just remember this: as highly sensitive and empathic people, thoughts and emotions are a big part of our purpose. That fantastically imaginative and *loud* mind, the ability to think and feel so deeply; these things weren't given to you for no reason.

The healer needs to learn to sit with painful emotions and let people feel heard with deep empathy. The creator needs to be able to dive into that emotionally rich world of imagination in order to create, and they also need to know how to come back up for air. The visionary needs to understand how to get out of their own head long enough to make a difference for others.

What you'll learn in the next chapter will take effort to implement, but you were born for this. We all have a job to do. So let's go.

---

1. Pert, Candace B. Molecules of Emotion: The Science Behind Mind-Body Medicine. Touchstone, 1999.

Chapter 7
Resilience & Reframing

"The world breaks everyone, and afterward, many are strong at the broken places." --- Ernest Hemingway

You might imagine someone who has practiced making friends with their thoughts for fifteen years would always be calm, cool, and collected. Not so much, friends. As I write this chapter, I'm dealing with my own tumultuous rumbles with emotion. Now, in my defense, I really am usually pretty calm and patient. I almost never channel my Italian grandmother (who once famously threw a Thanksgiving turkey down the stairs), but right now I'm basically feeling mad at the world. It might be hormones. It might be absorbing too much anger over the world's injustice and social issues. It might be general stress, or all of the above. Either way, I'm a wreck.

I've had to ban myself from Facebook, because right now I have the urge to verbally clobber anyone who offends my well-researched sensibilities, even knowing full well I will sound like a total jerk when it's said and done.

I just want to let you know, we all struggle. You aren't alone. Literally, every person, highly sensitive or not, has times of feeling like they're losing it.

Resilience means you know you will find a way to get past times like these.

(And I did get past it. I know, because I'm feeling sane again as I edit this chapter.)

We are all human and we all struggle. As HSPs, we feel and experience everything deeply, and we empaths have a little something extra added to the fray: the emotions of others. Lucky us! As if our own feelings weren't enough, we also get bonus feelings!

As we talked about in the last chapter, life is messy and complicated already, and being highly sensitive just adds another layer of complex flavor to our ooey-gooey cake of life.

Becoming resilient doesn't mean everything will be easy for us from here on out. It doesn't mean your cake of life isn't ever going to wobble. It doesn't even mean you're always going to have the balance needed to keep it from toppling over. But if your cake does fall and splat on the floor, well, you're going to pick it back up, brush the cat hair off, lick the frosting off your fingers, and carry on.

Of course, you can cry first. In fact, I highly recommend it.

And fine, if you're a germaphobe, you can bake a new one and *then* carry on. Fair enough?

One universally valuable tool I picked up in coaching school is called reframing. This is where we shift our viewpoint to see a situation in new ways. When we do that, we notice fresh possibilities. Like, "Oh, the bakery is open! I can buy a new cake. I don't have to serve this cat-hair covered one, after all."

Yes, sometimes solutions do become that obvious when we take a step back and look at the situation from new angles. Since there will always be multiple ways to view things, sometimes we just have to choose the story that brings us the most peace.

I have a little exercise in this chapter to help you put reframing to work in your own life, along with a couple of my favorite curated tips for when we feel stuck in our thought and feeling patterns. I think you'll see that a big part of resilience comes from how we tell our own stories, so let's start there.

The Importance of Stories

It's estimated that one-hundred billion people have lived on earth throughout history. Isn't it amazing that out of all of them, no one has ever lived your life story and no one ever will again? Your life is a once-in-history, never-to-be-repeated event! Kind of a big deal, huh?

But when you think of it, there are at least two versions of our life stories: 1) What happened on the outside of us (some might say, *"in reality"*), and 2) What happened inside of us (in our perception and response).

I think a lot of people would argue that reality is more important than our personal perception, but I'm proposing the idea that perception is actually more important.

Why? *Because your perception shapes your response, and can shift the rest of your story.*

As sensitive people, our perception is complicated. We notice small details others miss and process everything deeply. Empaths feel others' feelings, so a look or vibe of disappointment that might go right over someone else's head strikes at your heart. You might also have loud noises rattling your nerves, or feelings of uneasiness in a crowd. Experiences like these burrow down into your subconscious, leading you to later avoid situations where you might feel unsafe again.

Perhaps nothing terrible happened in reality, but our sensitive perception can make some everyday occurrences somewhat traumatic. Feeling everything so deeply can make the world seem like a scary, adversarial place—and sometimes it can be. The feelings you have are legitimate, but when our sensitive perception is driving us to live a life of fear and avoidance, something needs to change.

Does that seem true for you? Do you ever avoid doing things you'd like to do because of fear and being overwhelmed? Perhaps you have a preoccupation with "what people think," and are always trying to avoid that empathic gut-punch when they're suddenly unhappy?

If fear and avoidance are in the driver's seat, we can't live fully into our gifts of sensitivity. The good news is, we can shift our direction by changing the stories we tell ourselves—in other words, by reframing.

Let's say there is something you want to experience, but it scares the heck out of you. For example, when I was about nineteen, I remember making a phone call to a local college asking how to sign up for classes. The lady who answered told me I needed to go to the main campus in a city I wasn't familiar with. As she tried to give me directions and instructions, my head was spinning. I hung up the phone and just sobbed. The simplest task of driving somewhere new and finding my way around was completely overwhelming because I was telling myself a story that had me paralyzed with fear: I would get lost. That was literally the story. I couldn't sign up for classes, because I would get lost.

I would love to go back and talk to my younger self. I wish I could tell her how to change the story and get unstuck, but since I can't, I'll just tell you, instead.

When our minds come up with a story, we don't have to run with it. Oh, I know that fantastic imagination is ready and willing to play out a horrible scenario in your head, but the first thing to pop into the mind is only *one* possibility. It generally only seems so probable because our brains are matching it up with something that happened in our past, perhaps along with strong feelings that arose at the time. This is because when we have a traumatic experience (whether it be big or small), our brains are wired to avoid similar experiences in the future. This is a wonderful tool to keep us safe, but we have to know how to override it when necessary.

The Emergency Brake

When I was new to this thought wrangling thing, I learned a quick and handy trick that became something I often used to override fearful thinking. When your mind throws you a worst-case scenario story, you can stop it in its tracks by firmly saying, *"Cancel!"*

Do not let yourself chew on the idea for another second, and especially don't let yourself embody the feeling that goes with the thought.

I learned the "cancel" trick from motivational speaker Rita Davenport. She shared a relatable story about when her son started driving. While he was out, she would find horrific scenarios popping into her head. Car crashes. Police officers knocking at the door. Not things any parent wants to think of, but we all know how bad our imaginations can be. As soon as an awful story popped up, she began telling herself, *"Cancel!"* before it could go another theoretical inch.

It's true—we can die a thousand deaths and experience countless tragedies just by playing them out in our minds. We learned earlier in this book that we can't think about something without a chemical cascade being released in the body. Thoughts have power. So next time a worst case scenario punches you in the gut, try saying, *"Cancel, cancel, cancel!"* as many times as it takes.

Personally, I've been using Rita's "cancel" trick for about fifteen years, so I can give it my official seal of approval. Consider it an emergency brake you can pull whenever catastrophic thinking rears its ugly head.

The Clean Sweep

Another simple but important tool for changing your story is *changing your physiology*. As we've established, stories don't only happen in our heads; they trigger the molecules of emotion, which affect our entire bodies. So if you've been telling a sad or frightening story, those emotional peptides have been traveling throughout your body, giving you a physiology to match.

If you're only shifting your thoughts, your body may be slow to catch up. After all, it's still loaded with chemical messengers from your last experience. As a result, you can be thinking positive thoughts and "canceling" the negative ones, but your body may still be like, "Nope, things are still rotten!"

A quick way to realign yourself is to do something different with your body.

Notice your posture. Are you slouchy? How about your breath? Is it shallow, like you're in fight or flight mode?

These are things you can easily shift no matter where you are at, or who is around. Now, if you're in the comfort of your own home, you can really have some fun with changing your physiology. Turning on some music and dancing is my personal favorite way to change my mood. You can also just stand in a power pose [1], reaching your arms up in the air or putting them on your hips superhero style, all while taking some slow, deep breaths.

Going for a brisk walk or run is another option. Getting your body moving helps flush the old sad molecules out while getting some feel-good ones flowing. By the way, this tip comes from none other than author and motivational speaker Tony Robbins. I told you I've studied the work of all the classic personal improvement dudes.

OK, so you now know how to cancel a nasty story and how to clear it out of your body. Use the cancel trick when your imagination is taking you to dark places you don't want to go. Change your physiology when you're just feeling down in the dumps. These are great tools for counteracting fear-based thinking and Negative-Nellying. But think of it this way: do you pull the emergency brake every time you need to stop your car? How about getting out the power washer each night to do dishes?

Obviously we don't always want to go for the nuclear option, right? In the same way, it wouldn't be healthy for your system to use these tools every time you have an unpleasant thought or feeling. Dr. Candace Pert said this in *Molecules of Emotion: The Science Behind Mind-Body Medicine:*

My research has shown me that when emotions are expressed—which is to say that the biochemicals that are the substrate of emotion are flowing freely—all systems are united and made whole. When emotions are repressed, denied, and not allowed to be whatever they may be, our network pathways get blocked, stopping the flow of the vital feel-good, unifying chemicals that run both our biology and behavior.[2]

Every day, we have thoughts and emotions that serve a purpose. The point isn't to squash and power wash them off into oblivion with constant dancing and power poses. Freely feeling emotions is healthy and necessary. We need both emotions and thoughts as our allies, guiding us in ways that support our gifts.

So, I'm going to walk you through five steps for making friends with your thoughts and emotions. Here, we aren't going to run from them. Instead, we're going to listen to what they are saying, process what needs to be processed, and reframe what has us feeling stuck.

Get out your journal and really work on these steps. And get excited about creating some amazing shifts in the way you think and experience life.

5 Steps for Making Friends With Your Thoughts & Emotions

1: Notice: Our first step in making friends with our thoughts is simply to notice them. Often we're in survival mode, with our thoughts and emotions swirling uncontrollably as we push through each day. We hardly stop to take a breath, let alone be introspective about our reactions.

So I invite you to practice noticing your thoughts and emotions by asking yourself:

- *What are you thinking about throughout your day?*
- *What feelings are connected with those thoughts? (For example, are you feeling afraid, angry, sad, ashamed, lonely, empty, or overwhelmed?)*
- *Is there a predominant theme threading throughout your experience?*
- *Are you feeling the molecules of emotion in your body, and if so, where? It could be a tightness or tension in the jaw, back, or neck, discomfort in your belly, or something else.*

No judgment or push to change is needed at this stage. Just observe the reactions in your body. Keep in mind that sometimes when we stop to notice and feel, the emotions feel more intense for a time. It's more than OK to cry and let those molecules flow freely.

Do this step for a couple of days before moving on.

2: Reflect: Look back at the predominant emotions (or feelings) you've been experiencing and noting in step one. List them out if you haven't yet. (Again, use feeling words such as afraid, angry, sad, ashamed, etc.)

Now ask yourself, with each one: *What is this emotion here to tell me?*

Remember, emotions are messengers of change. True, sometimes you *can't* change things, but you can always accept the message that you want something to be different.

Let those little molecules of emotion be heard and felt in the body. Whatever you think they are trying to tell you, journal it out.

3: Shift: Now that you have the message, ask yourself: *What do I need to do next?* Does something need to shift in your life?

If we don't learn the lessons our emotions are trying to teach us, we can end up stuck.

Sometimes the message of change is going to feel overwhelming. If so, don't overthink it. If we get stuck in our heads, nothing changes, and the emotions will keep jabbing at us into eternity.

If you're struggling, it may help to distill it down. *What is the smallest, most doable action step that can move me in the right direction?*

Make a plan to take that first step.

4: Release: Sometimes things are not changeable, or are not within our power to change at the moment. When we can't change something, often there is a tendency to ruminate on it. It is as if our brains believe that, by playing it over and over ad nauseam, the situation might change.

Well, believe me, I've tried chewing on negative thoughts day in and day out, and it doesn't change a thing—except possibly deepening the lines in my forehead. This is where journaling can help us release and reframe the things we can't control.

If you're prone to ruminate, get in the habit of asking: *Is this thought serving me?*

If the answer is *"No,"* please don't try to justify it—like, *"No, but he did this to me and so I have no choice..."* Stop there, friend. With thoughts, you always have a choice. They are *your* thoughts!

Still, we need to process whatever is going on. Put your pen to paper and ask yourself these ques*tions:*

1. *What is true about this situation?*
2. *What else might be true?*

For example, perhaps you're upset with someone. *It's true* they acted rude and inconsiderate, and maybe *it's true* you have every right to be upset. But it could *also be true* that the other person's reaction had more to do with them than it did with you. It could *also be true* that they were under stress and having a bad day. It could *also be true* that their opinion doesn't change who you are.

Asking *"What is true?"* helps us process our feelings and release their emotional charge. In line with what Dr. Pert said, when we let our emotions be what they are, we allow the energy in our bodies to flow properly. Asking *"What else might be true?"* reframes the situation and helps us come to peace with it.

By the way, these are also the questions I would ask the young me, who was so frightened of getting lost. *What was true?* Google Maps didn't exist back then. It was true that I could have gotten lost. *What else might have been true?* It might have been true that I could have asked for help. A lot of times our stories tell us we can't get help, don't they? It also might have been true that I was strong enough to do hard things, and could have found my way home even if I did get lost. But alas, that was a story that would take a long time to learn.

5: Affirm: When I say I "affirm" I mean it's time to create an affirmation. An affirmation is a statement that something is true. The catch is, our affirmations are aspirational, so they aren't true—yet. The statement you're going to create will tell your brain a new story, one that embodies the feeling and experience you want in your life. Once you have your affirmation ready, you will keep it handy and state it out loud to yourself several times a day.

Maybe you feel like it's silly idea to talk to yourself, but truth is, you're already talking to yourself—and reinforcing neural pathways—all the livelong day. With affirmations, the only difference is that you're consciously choosing to tell a story that builds you up, instead of passively listening to the subconscious stories trying to tear you down.

To create your affirmation, try asking:
1. *How do I want to feel?*
2. *What do I want the outcome of this situation to be?*
3. *What do I do to get there?*

For example, say you've been experiencing a lot of frustration about your body and know you've been neglecting self-care:
1. *How do you want to feel? You might answer: happy and strong.*
2. *What outcome do you want? To become healthier and more confident.*
3. *What do you need to do? Eat well and move your body.*

The resulting affirmation for this example could be, *"I am so happy to feel healthy, strong, and confident. Each day I feed and move my body with care."*

Affirmations should always be stated in the present tense, like you already have what you want. If you just say "I want to" or "in the future I will", it creates a feeling of longing and lack. And let's face it, we've likely already been telling ourselves that we will do something someday. To create change, we have to tell our minds something different. The best kind of affirmation is phrased in a way that gives you a feeling of gratitude and contentment. Using phrases like *"I'm so thankful for..."* or *"I'm so excited that...."* can be very effective.

When we speak with feeling, as if we already are in our desired state, our minds are listening. The subconscious perks up and thinks, "Oh, we are doing that now? Well, it feels pretty good. Yes, it feels safe and cozy. Okay, I'm in!" Practical, present tense affirmations get the brain on board with your plans.

Now that you have your affirmation, you'll want to put it somewhere you can see it on a regular basis. One idea is to create a wallpaper for your phone with the affirmation on it. Good old sticky notes are another way to do it. You can place them on your bathroom mirror, your desk, or even the fridge. Make it a practice to say your affirmation out loud, several times a day, trying to embody the positive feeling it would give you to be living in your desired experience. At the very least, put a sticky note on your bathroom mirror and say your affirmation aloud several times as you get ready in the morning and before you go to sleep at night.

With your affirmations in place, your mind will work to align your actions to create the desired reality you speak of.

By the way, this isn't brainwashing! We're simply creating new neural pathways. These pathways allow your brain to be on board with doing what you were made to do in the first place. In an ideal world, you would have been taught to think in a way that benefited you. For many of us, that isn't how life played out. We picked up many untrue and limiting beliefs about ourselves and what we are capable of. You have every right—even the responsibility—to teach yourself how to think and act in alignment with who you really are.

Obviously, creating new neural pathways doesn't happen overnight. It takes time, so this isn't something you just do a couple of times and forget about (At least not if you want it to work!). The more you tell the story, the more your subconscious mind will align with it, and the easier it will be to take action.

Remember, we all tell stories. Make yours a good one. The reality of the past doesn't change, but by giving ourselves a new perspective, we can change the story, shift our response, and shape the future.

So there you have it, a simple five-step process for making friends with your thoughts and emotions. In reality, of course, it never feels so simple—it feels more like picking cat hair out of frosting as you squish that broken cake back together. But if you make a habit of processing your thoughts through these emotionally grounding questions, it really does create transformation.

Are you feeling resistant to giving this a whirl? Sometimes we don't want to let go of our emotions. Maybe life has been kind of rotten to us, and we rationalize that we're entitled to wallow. Or maybe people in our lives have been rather awful, and we worry that if we stop being angry we just might be letting someone off the hook who doesn't deserve it.

I think most of us have been in that place at some time or another. And you know what? You have every right to wallow. Eat that entire pint of ice cream (been there) and zone out in front of Netflix for a while. No one would blame you. But does it serve you or your higher purpose to ruminate on all the things, all the time?

Sooner or later, you have to rise back up. You're a person of purpose, remember? You hold the gifts of sensitivity, your special secret sauce. If you are stuck, someone who needs your gifts is going to be stuck, too.

So do what you need to do, remember who you are, and readjust your crown. Resilience means you will always rise in the end.

By the way, in this chapter, we have pretty much just talked about light scenarios when nothing really bad has *actually* happened. Of course, that isn't always the case. Our fears and patterns of avoidance can be deeply rooted in trauma. When this is the case, it can be harder to break those negative patterns. Sometimes we feel broken, but as the saying goes, broken crayons still color. No one can replace the beautiful color you bring to the picture. You are truly worth fighting for.

Also, don't be afraid to ask for help. There are therapists and practitioners out there who are trained to address stored trauma. No, they don't erase what happened, but they can help you take the emotional charge out of the memories so you can move forward.

Emotional Freedom Technique (EFT), Aroma Freedom Technique (AFT), and Somatic Experiencing are other tools that helped me a great deal. I don't think I'd be writing this book without them. Don't give up on finding something that works for you. Use the tools in this chapter to start exploring, and if you need to, seek out whatever other resources you need.

In the next chapter, we're going to talk about the feelings of anxiety and being overwhelmed that sensitive, empathic people often experience. So lick that frosting off your fingers and turn the page.

---

1. http://nrs.harvard.edu/urn-3:HUL.InstRepos:9547823
2. Pert, Candace B. "Chapter 12: Healing Feeling, Section: Body Psychotherapy." Molecules of Emotion: The Science Behind Mind-Body Medicine, Touchstone, New York, NY, 1999, p. 273.

Chapter 8

Anxiety & Overwhelm

"Nobody realizes that some people expend tremendous energy merely to be normal." --- Albert Camus

If you remember back in Chapter 2, we talked about the characteristics of highly sensitive people as defined by Dr. Elaine Aron. One of those characteristics is being *easily overstimulated*.

We process everything going on around us at a deeper level than most, and that, my friends, is exhausting. We might assume we just aren't very resilient people, since we get worn out quicker than most. Or we may come to the conclusion that something is truly wrong with us. Maybe we've even been told something *is wrong* about us by someone we respect.

Highly sensitive people are often diagnosed with things like chronic fatigue, depression, and anxiety, both because we aren't well understood and because an out-of-balance nervous system really can throw the body out of whack.

For example, I recently saw an infographic on ADHD and was surprised how perfectly the description could have been describing the feeling of being overwhelmed that highly sensitive people often experience. I could see how an HSP (especially as a child) could be mislabeled by well-meaning people who are only looking at behavior and missing what's really going on inside.

Being sensitive may be your superpower, but remember, even Superman had his Kryptonite. We have to be aware that a chronically overstimulated nervous system can wreak havoc on the body.

As highly sensitive people, what's easy peasy for someone else may be demanding and stressful to us, and as we know, prolonged stress isn't good for our bodies.

When we're under stress, our nervous system sends messages to the body that are designed to get us pumped up and ready to run for our lives. Even though our modern stressors usually don't require outrunning a predator, the physical response we experience is the same: our heart rate and breathing speed up, our blood pressure increases, and hormones such as adrenaline and cortisol are released to provide us with immediate energy. Blood flow is routed away from digestion to the arms and legs (because if a bear is chasing you, quick limbs are more important than a properly digested sandwich).

Ideally, the stress would pass quickly and we'd return to our normal relaxed state of being, but for some of us, the "rest and digest" phase rarely comes.

Many of us live in an almost constant state of stress. This is especially true if you've experienced trauma, which could have wired your brain for constant fight or flight, giving you an unending edgy feeling of vigilance. You're always waiting for the other shoe to drop.

When this is the case, our digestion is consistently compromised — we aren't properly absorbing nutrients, our gut bacteria are thrown off balance, and we can even develop a leaky gut. In addition, our poor adrenal glands eventually get exhausted from pumping out all those stress hormones, which could lead to brain fog, chronic exhaustion, and weight gain. This can lead to you being further unable to deal with seemingly minor stressors.

If any of this sounds familiar, you might want to find a functional medicine or integrative health practitioner in your area. These are doctors who know how to test for and treat things like leaky gut and adrenal insufficiency. I've chosen this kind of doctor for myself and my family because they really listen and are trained to get to the root of the problem. Best of all, they won't tell you it's all in your head, which is pretty refreshing.

So now that we've covered the feeling of being overwhelmed, what about anxiety or depression, clinically diagnosed or otherwise? These are things many highly sensitive people struggle with. Perhaps all too often, doctors jump straight to prescribing meds without figuring out the underlying cause.

In her book, *The Empath's Survival Guide,* Dr. Judith Orloff talks about how empaths are often very sensitive to medications. She says if empaths do need a prescription, they generally only need a very small dose.[1] If you do feel medication is necessary, look for a doctor who will work with you as an individual, because nothing is one size fits all.

We definitely won't be treating any diseases in this book, but we will be talking about how highly sensitive people can best manage stress and try to combat feelings of anxiety and depression. When we enable our bodies to relax and feel safe, we are giving our bodies space to work on healing.

As highly sensitive people, we might not be completely aware of everyday things triggering our stress response. After all, others may have told us this stuff is "no big deal," so we try to brush it off and power through. On the other hand, there are probably triggers you are all too well aware of.

Either way, we need to be conscious of what sets off our nervous systems. Only then can we learn how to mitigate the stress response. We can't totally avoid stress, but we can learn to deal with overstimulating circumstances in a healthier way.

As we learn how to do this, you'll be able to step back and reframe, to see your own triggers (such as thoughts like, "My friends will hate me if I don't go to the football game!" or, "The kids will be disappointed if we don't see everything at Disney!") from a different viewpoint. This lets you detach from all the emotional goo that goes along with trying to avoid anxiety and overwhelming feelings.

Right now there's no pressure, so it's a good time to think about how (or whether) you want to manage your triggers differently in the future. We're going to list out eight situations that can easily push our highly sensitive nervous systems into overwhelm. See which ones you relate to the most. This section is focused on situations when you have a choice. Later we'll talk about how to avoid burnout when you have no choice but to power through.

Top Eight HSP Stress Triggers

#1 Getting Hangry:

Who else feels hungry, and then feels angry about five seconds later?

About halfway through writing this book, I got the idea to do a cleanse along with some intermittent fasting. The thing about cleanses, as we all know, is at the beginning you are hungry. It's a little miserable until the metabolism finally agrees to give in and burn some fat.

By the second day of my cleanse, I had spent about six hours staring at the computer screen and only had three sentences to show for it. Apparently, my brain staunchly refuses to spit out any words unless it is fed.

Alas, this book is brought to you by almond butter toast and stretchy pants.

Being hungry is a stressor, and low blood sugar is downright miserable. Plan nourishing meals at regular intervals, and bring snacks as needed (this is coming from a girl who usually has at least one squished protein bar at the bottom of her purse). A prepared HSP is a happy HSP.

#2 Being in a Rush:

When you are rushed, do you freeze up or make poor decisions? Sometimes we feel stupid because of this, but we shouldn't berate ourselves. Our nervous systems are just overwhelmed by the frantic energy of rushing, and when that happens, we can't process information quickly enough.

When I'm rushed, I'm prone to channel my Italian grandmother (remember the one who threw the turkey down the stairs?).

When my kids were little, I decided I was not going down in history like that, so I learned to avoid being rushed. I also hate being late, so I just started getting ready for things ridiculously early. But little kids are gonna take 5,000 hours just to put on shoes, and then they'll have forgotten to brush their teeth—you know the drill. Once you finally get out of the house you're driving like Carroll Shelby with adrenaline through the roof, screaming like a lunatic as you hit every single red light.

Or is that just me?

Anyway, sometimes things happen and we can't avoid it, but if you *can* arrange your schedule to avoid rushing, your sensitive nervous system will thank you for it.

#3 Crowds of People:

I think you already know this one, right? Highly sensitive people usually hate crowds. Being in a herd of people produces a lot of anxiety for many of us.

And yet, we may feel bad about ourselves for feeling so bad. I know I used to be embarrassed about how crowds overwhelmed and exhausted me so much. Everyone else would be like, "Wasn't that amazing?" after a concert or other big event, while I was often thinking, "No, are you kidding? It was miserable, and I felt like sardines in a can."

Still, I'd just smile and nod, thinking it was just me. But you know what? It wasn't.

Once I started sharing that crowds give me the heebie-jeebies, I found a lot of people felt similarly—especially depending on the vibe of the event. After all, a crowded Bible study convention and a crowded boxing match don't have the same feel, do they?

As sensitives, we generally have a distaste for being anywhere aggressive energy permeates. We aren't the ones to quickly jump on board with a crowd mentality. Our intuition tells us, "No, this is not our vibe!" Consider that a good thing.

Even when a crowd has great, positive energy, it's totally possible to be overstimulated by the intensity of the experience. Especially for those of us who are empaths, remember that constantly scanning and absorbing emotions is draining.

This is something people with less sensitive nervous systems cannot understand, because their experience with crowds is quite different. We can't get stuck worrying too much about what non-HSPs think. Trying to explain how you can feel electromagnetic energy and they can't will probably not go over too well.

It's OK. You don't have to explain yourself. It's fine to leave early, go out to the car, or retreat to the bathroom. It's also OK to say "No" if you don't want or need to go in the first place. Do what you need to do to take care of your nervous system.

#4 Conflicts, Arguing, and Yelling (oh my!):

You know how I said I wanted to be a lawyer? Well, part of the reason was that I really like to argue. My favorite things in school were mock trials and debates.

The funny thing is, I hate conflict! But at the same time, it's hard for me to resist a good intellectual throw down.

OK, so my point in sharing this with you is not to make you think I'm an argumentative jerk, but to teach you a fine lesson in *sensation seeking*.

Sometimes we crave things that give our nervous systems a little buzz of energy. We may enjoy the sensation of something like debating (particularly when we fancy ourselves good at winning, *ahem*) but in the long run, it probably isn't very good for us. We wind up overstimulated, having internalized too much negative energy and worked our nervous systems into a tizzy.

With social media being the way it is, we could literally spend all day, every day arguing politics and ethics with friends or strangers. We may even find a little thrill in it, but you have to ask: is this worth the energy I am expending? Also, what energy am I absorbing? Is it frantic and angry?

Most of us realize in-person arguing is incredibly draining, but online arguments can be just as detrimental to our well-being. Of course, sometimes we have to speak up for truth and justice—we can't forget the calling of the visionary. But choosing our battles is very important. If you find yourself getting sucked into conflict on a regular basis, it may be a good idea to stay away from whoever or whatever is pulling you in (Did I hear someone whisper "*Facebook*"?)

#5 Boom, Crash, Bang:

"For the love of all that is holy, keep it down!"

Does anyone else say this at least three times a day? If so, you just might be a highly sensitive person with children.

Whether you have kids or not, as an HSP, you probably find that loud sounds quickly wear on your nerves.

For example, my dishwasher makes the most annoying beeping sound when it's done running (I should have a better example, but nope, I'm here whining about my dishwasher). I wish I had something to measure the decibels of that thing, because it's ridiculous. I also wish there was some way to turn it off, because I literally feel it in my chest every time it goes off. We feel loud sounds in our bodies, and the sensation can feel quite jarring and unpleasant.

If we're at a party with a loud bass vibrating the room, a game where people are obnoxiously whoop-whooping over the voices and music blaring through the speakers, or—heaven forbid, a monster truck rally, we may have a hard time shaking the buzzy feeling from our nervous system.

Particularly when combined with crowds, loud noises can leave a sensitive person feeling on edge for quite some time afterward. If you've felt silly or alone because loud sounds irritate you so much, you're not. The effect of sound on your nervous system is real.

#6 Synthetic Scents and Toxic Yuck:

Having a more sensitive nervous system often makes us more aware of what is affecting our bodies. We might be the first to get a headache when someone is wearing too much perfume, or perhaps we can't stand to walk down the cleaning aisle at the supermarket because the stench is so overpowering.

Many of us know, instinctively or through research, that synthetic chemicals aren't good for our health. And as we already discussed, our body systems can be struggling enough without adding toxins into the mix!

Everyone would benefit from reducing their synthetic chemical exposure. As a sensitive person, you might just have an even greater sense of well-being when you get the toxins out of your home and off your body.

#7 Dealing with Clutter:

I imagine the ancient Chinese people who came up with Feng Shui must have been highly sensitive. They knew that the way their environment was arranged affected their energy and how they felt. It was probably much easier back then, since they didn't have to deal with daily junk mail deliveries, plastic kids' toys, or storing seasonal clothing and decor.

Hey, I may know intuitively that being surrounded by clutter is overstimulating and clear surfaces make me calm, but this doesn't mean I am good at keeping things neat.

Right now, my desk is covered in receipts, bills, coupons I probably won't remember to use, kids' drawings, colored pencils, a book on the autonomic nervous system, my son's school books, a box of notecards, a roll of packing tape, new insurance cards I didn't put in my wallet yet, a broken diffuser, and an empty paper bag.

And it's not that big of a desk.

Guys, I am no Marie Kondo. I am your slightly disorganized and brutally honest friend Jennifer, who will never tell you I have it all together when I don't. I will tell you I need to take a break from writing and clean up this mess so I can think straight.

The highly sensitive brain doesn't need any extra stuff to take in. Knowing this, we can be more aware and do our best to keep the clutter monster at bay.

#8 Too Much Peopling:

As HSPs, our nervous systems need regular breaks from stimulation to recover. Whether we are introverted or extroverted, we need our alone time.

In addition, as described by Dr. Elaine Aron, most of us are very intuitive. Our brains need quiet time to take all the information we've gathered and weave it together. Peace and quiet are fuel for the intuitive mind. Without them, intuitives feel stuck, frustrated, and overwhelmed.

As a child, I understood this about myself. I was quite happy to be left alone in my room to think, draw, and write. But as an adult, particularly as a parent, my boundaries got squishy.

I felt like I should be available to my family twenty-four hours a day, seven days a week, with no breaks. That's kind of the job description of being a parent, because kids can need you at any time, day or night. Still, I discovered (the hard way, as usual) that if I didn't plan quiet time for myself, I was constantly burnt out and too mentally fatigued to be fully present.

Even if you don't have kids, you can find yourself overwhelmed by a jam-packed, people-filled schedule. If your interactions with people wind up being negative or just too much, they can leave you with an anxious and overwhelmed feeling that is hard to shake.

We need to learn to take breaks, step away, and say no as needed in order to protect our physical and mental well-being.

We also need to remember that social media is not alone time. It's another one of those sensory-seeking behaviors that feels kind of good, but still leaves us buzzing with overstimulation. While it can be a fun way to connect with friends, don't use up all your precious alone time scrolling, OK?

Moving On —

There you have it: eight ways to slowly drive a highly sensitive person nuts. We'd better not let our enemies know about this, huh?

By the way, the HSP stress triggers were listed in no particular order. Everyone is different, and we all have things that bother us more than others. It doesn't mean anything is wrong with us—it's just our highly sensitive nervous systems trying to deal with modern life.

Before you move on, grab your journal and get your thoughts out on paper. Under this chapter's heading you'll find questions to help you clarify what stresses you out and how best you can deal with it.

Of course, we can't totally avoid or control what stresses us. Sometimes we are just in the thick of it and have to power through. It's OK. We want to live fully, not as hermits locked in soundproof rooms, right? (If you're not sure, the answer is, *"Yes, right. Hermitting is only a 'sometimes' thing."*)

Remember your gifts of sensitivity. We need you to be seen and heard, and that means you need tools to cope with your high sensitivity before your nerves start to feel like grated cheese.

Next, let's talk about some simple ways to take back control of the nervous system and avoid burnout. Want to know what tip number one is? Of course you do! Turn the page...

---

1. Orloff, Judith. The Empath's Survival Guide: Life Strategies for Sensitive People. Sounds True, Inc., 2018.

Chapter 9

Life, Breath, and the PNS

"Live in each season as it passes; breathe the air, drink the drink, taste the fruit, and resign yourself to the influence of the earth." --- Henry David Thoreau, Walden

Are you ready to hear the best and simplest way to take control of your nervous system and avoid burnout? It is...drumroll...wait for it, wait for it—
Breathing.
Ta da!
Man, despite my silly attempt to jazz things up, it's hard to make breathing sound exciting. I mean it's just breathing, after all.
Bear with me though, OK? I know you already know a good deal about breathing, since you've been doing it since birth, and all. I,

too, have been taking in oxygen for a good many years—but it was only a short time ago I learned the importance of *how* we breathe.

Here is the scoop on breathing, just in case no one bothered to tell you, either. This will be a quick chapter, but don't be tempted to skip ahead. Breathing is way more interesting than it sounds. Besides, I'm going to throw you a few even more exciting tips for calming the nervous system at the end. Fair enough?

In our last chapter, we talked about how, when we experience stress, the nervous system sends messages to put us into what we know as "fight or flight" mode. This is the sympathetic branch of the autonomic nervous system in action.

You don't need to remember this, and there will be no quiz, I promise. But if you'd like to nerd out with me for a moment I think you'll find the knowledge valuable. After all, as a sensitive person, your nervous system is kind of a big deal.

To remember what the autonomic nervous system (ANS) does, you may want to think of it as "automatic." Autonomic equals automatic. Simple, right?

You don't have to think about the ANS working; it just does its thing. We don't have to remember to make our heart pump or blood flow or lungs breathe, thank goodness. The autonomic nervous system keeps all those necessary functions—and more—regulated and chugging along.

In addition, there are two branches of this system which work in opposite ways to keep us balanced. First, we have the sympathetic branch (SNS), which responds quickly and gets us mobilized for action. The SNS is the part we talked about in the last chapter that causes blood to move away from the gut and toward the limbs so we can quickly run from a bear.

Except maybe our "bear" is a grumpy customer who keeps sending nasty emails, or a jackhammer in a nearby construction zone.

If our silly bears would just go away, the other branch of the nervous system, called the parasympathetic (PNS), could kick in.

The parasympathetic part works more slowly, dampening the responses of the sympathetic. It slows down the heart rate and breathing and turns digestion back on.

But if those bears are always breathing down our necks, our body doesn't get the message we are safe, our PNS doesn't dampen the responses, and we find ourselves chronically unable to relax, rest, and digest. Over time, this really wears on the body.

But here's the good news you've been waiting for: *There are simple things we can do to send the PNS the message that it's safe to chill.*

As mentioned, probably the simplest and most effective way to accomplish this is by paying attention to your breath. The great thing about breathing is that it's pretty much always available to you. All heck could be breaking loose, but you will still have your breath as a tool.

Of course, when something is so easy to do, it's also easy *not* to do. Even though breathing exercises are simple, your brain is used to doing things a certain way. It's going to take conscious thought and discipline to retrain yourself. If you've been stuck in perpetual fight or flight, you may be used to shallow breathing. Perhaps you even tend to breathe through your mouth more than your nose. When you start to take deeper breaths it can feel strange, or like you can't get enough air in. However, for most of us with healthy airways and lungs, when we keep practicing connecting with our breath, it gets easier.

But first things first. The goal of working with your breathing should not be to force your body to do something. Your body is wise and (shocker) already knows how to breathe. That means, if your breath is fast or slow or shallow or deep, there's a reason behind it.

Therefore, it's better to start with noticing and *connecting with* your body, rather than attempting to change it. When we're aware of our breath and present in our body, that, in itself, begins to calm the nervous system.

As with anything, listen to your body. What's right for one isn't right for everyone. For example, if your nervous system is in another state called "freeze" (which may feel like depression), slowing your breathing isn't going to pull you in the right direction. Freeze is the state of shock an animal goes into when it senses impending death. If you're stuck in a functional freeze, slowing down your breathing is like telling yourself, "Hey, I think I'll relax a little more as this bear chews my arm off."

Probably not a good move. If this sounds like you (minus the bear attack), something more invigorating would likely be a better choice.

Anyway, this chapter is *not* meant to prescribe you a protocol of personalized breathing exercises. It is to let you know that your breath can be a key to regulating your nervous system. You can always tap into your intuition and explore what makes you feel better.

Calming Tool #1: An Example Breathing Exercise

One possible exercise to start with is the 5-5-7 breath. This is the one I was taught in coaching school, but there are many variations, including the 4-7-8 breath. I will use 5-5-7 for an example but feel free to adjust to what is comfortable for your body. You can do this anywhere, but preferably get in a comfortable position and take a moment to let your shoulders and neck relax. (The time to start practicing breathing is not when you're already freaking out.)

Inhale through your nose for a count of five, hold for five, then exhale out of your nose for a count of seven. Do this at least ten times, for a total of about two minutes.

Provided you feel ready, go ahead. Give it a whirl. I'll wait!

Now, wasn't that pretty easy and relaxing?

Of course, you can find countless methods of breathwork online. One I recently discovered is the Wim Hof Method, which combines both breathing exercises and cold therapy to strengthen the nervous system and body overall (you can check it out at www.wimhofmethod.com). Wim Hof is an extraordinary fellow known as the "Iceman" who is known for doing fun stuff like running a half marathon above the Arctic Circle, barefoot and wearing only shorts.

I'm not even sure if my fried adrenals can handle walking to the mailbox in December without a sweater, but still, it's interesting to explore what our bodies might be capable of when we learn to control our breath.

So, if you're anything like me, you're excited to incorporate breathwork into your routine, but will probably forget about it by next week. No worries. We can get around the natural tendency to forget by anchoring our new habit to something we already do, like eating (once again, if you're like me, eating is not something you're going to forget to do). With this in mind, a great time to practice your breathing is before each meal.

Why? Because when we breathe slowly and deeply, we're signaling our nervous systems to rest and digest. Many of us are spending ghastly amounts of money on supplements and organic, nutrient-dense food, only to be unable to properly assimilate it because our digestive systems are too stressed to work properly.

So frustrating, isn't it? If you feel like you do everything right with eating clean and exercising yet still don't see great results, it's possible being stuck in a fight/flight/freeze state is at the root of the problem. Try making a habit of practicing the 5-5-7 breath, or your breathing exercise of choice, before you eat. As you breathe, take in the sight and smell of your food. Think about how fortunate you are to be able to fill your belly and nourish your body, including a prayer of gratitude if you are so inclined. Be present, chewing slowly and really tasting each bite. Pay attention to how your body is responding and stop before you're stuffed. (And yes, this all requires detaching from our phones during mealtime.) Incorporating these little practices during our meals can really improve how our bodies rest and digest.

I think we can all see how important it is to care for our nervous systems, particularly as the proud owners of highly sensitive ones. Again, we are faced with the fact that what works for most people doesn't always work for us. We may need a little more gentle care than those with less sensitive nervous systems.

Remember, this isn't because we're weak; it's just because we're wired differently. Neglecting our needs only leads to overwhelm, burnout, and health issues. So, beyond breathing, let's talk about a few additional ways we can support and calm the unique type of nervous system we've been blessed with.

Calming Tool #2: Gentle Movement

When something is out of whack in your body, have you noticed the tendency to want to "whip yourself into shape?"

We might imagine (as we have been told) that the only way to elicit a desired response from these pesky bodies is through forceful discomfort. Sometimes, forceful discomfort does get us visible results, at least temporarily, because the body will adapt to stress and deprivation in certain predictable ways.

But some of us find these robotically prescribed formulas of input and output don't equal the results we are told we should get!

Well, that's because something is lacking in the equation: *Healing*.

It's funny how our bodies were made to heal, and yet almost no one talks about it. One might imagine the body *can't* heal anything more than a scrape, at least not without modern interventions. Most current "health" paradigms (prescription or over-the-counter meds, or even supplements) are based on an outside force being exerted upon the body. Or an inside force, if you consider willpower, which your subconscious will always override if the thing you are trying to do feels unsafe or uncomfortably unfamiliar.

It's almost as if our bodies are viewed as the enemy, like they're just sitting around waiting to self-destruct and kill us. Isn't that silly? The body just wants to be well—and guess what? *It already knows how.*

It's true. Our bodies are wonderfully designed to heal and maintain a healthy balance. Just think of the amazingness of cell turnover, neuroplasticity, and homeostasis! Your body is always working hard to keep you alive and well.

And we see that in the autonomic nervous system, right? Fight or flight is balanced by rest and digest—in other words, healing. That is, it's balanced until we get a bit too far out of whack, which is when we need a little extra effort to correct things. We aren't powerless in this endeavor by any means, but we do have to be aware of what we're doing.

Imagine our highly sensitive nervous systems getting stuck in fight/flight/freeze, leading to our adrenal glands being exhausted from pumping out stress hormones all the livelong day. As a result, our bodies are feeling tired and puffy, and maybe getting a bit rounder than we'd like. What should we do to regain balance?

Maybe we should start getting up extra early to spend an hour at Crossfit? Perhaps start training for a half marathon?

Well, you may want to do those things eventually, if they appeal to you. But—as many of us have found out the hard way—*you can't fix the damage from stress by exerting more stress.*

Healing has to be accomplished before we can successfully build strength. If you try to skip that foundational step, your new exercise program may be a giant exercise in frustration.

We all know, generally speaking, that exercise is good for us, but we tend to assume this means doing more of it, in longer sessions with higher intensity, will only compound the benefits. That isn't always true.

We all need to move, but sometimes we need movement that is more gentle than punishing. Maybe that gentle movement is a walk, some stretching, or just dancing around the living room. The great thing is, when we allow ourselves to move gently, we also allow more time and energy for our bodies to heal. We can also be more consistent because by being gentle we avoid hitting the brick wall of burnout.

Are you getting stronger from your rituals of movement, or are you just going through the hustle/push/crash/burn/try-again cycle? If it's the latter, why not let yourself experience something different? It's just a matter of finding the ideal amount and intensity of movement for your unique self.

The first step to doing this is just becoming aware of our bodies and how we are really feeling. Many HSPs (particularly visionaries and creatives) spend a lot of time stuck in our heads. This tendency toward the cerebral can lead to a disconnection from our physical bodies. Even just noticing how our feet feel on the ground or our bottoms feel in our chair is a start!

As you become more connected with how your body feels, you're also going to become more aware of what your body needs. These needs are probably not going to be a surprise to you. After all, our bodies have been trying to tell us all along what we need to heal. We just don't always listen very well.

I know this is the case with me. I have always known that dance is very healing for me. When I'm dancing, every cell in my body feels happy. And yet, how many hours have I slogged on the treadmill, and how much money have I sunk into gym memberships and workout programs to "whip" me into shape?

I don't want to know the actual answer, but trust me when I say it was too many and too much.

Of course, there's no use crying over what we've done or not done with our bodies in the past, is there? Wasted membership fees and dusty ThighMasters from 1995 are part of many sad stories of disconnection from our bodies (although, at least the ThighMaster wasn't too hard on the old nervous system).

The good news is, right now, we can choose to truly love and care for our bodies. We can finally tune in and give them the type of healing movement they've been craving all along.

So, what do you really need? Maybe you also love to dance, or maybe you know you'd feel wonderful after a quiet, relaxing walk. And hey, maybe today all you need is to go lay in the sun or take a long, guilt-free nap. Remember, the body knows the answer. *Just listen*. Your sensitive nervous system will thank you!

Calming Tool #3: Connection with Nature

This one is so obvious, but sometimes ridiculously difficult! As much as we know being in nature is good for us, and we recognize it's very calming to the nervous system, our modern lives often keep us busy indoors or driving around. It's unfortunate, but not everyone has easy access to a relaxing spot outdoors.

Many of us live in a constant state of nature deprivation—and just think about how unnatural this really is! Our bodies were made to be outside, in contact with the earth. Of course I'm as thankful as anyone when it's cold and rainy and I have the luxury of staying in a toasty, warm house, but as nice as modern conveniences are, our bodies still crave what only sun, earth, and fresh air can provide.

Not as if your intuition needed further confirmation, but just in case, researchers at the Brighton and Sussex Medical School found that "playing 'natural sounds' affects the bodily systems that control the flight-or-fright and rest-digest autonomic nervous systems, with associated effects in the resting activity of the brain."[1]

Permission to play outside: granted.

Truly, I realize access to relaxing in nature is a luxury some don't have. Being physically able to play and work outside is a privilege not to be taken for granted. That being said, do what you can with what you have available to you.

Personally, I find hiking is almost a meditative activity—maybe because when you're trying not to trip over tree roots it's hard to worry about anything else. Perhaps you'd prefer something where you're less likely to twist an ankle, like gardening. Being able to take part in growing some of your own food is the ultimate reconnection with nature.

Of course, who says you have to *do* anything? Why not just step into the fresh air and breathe, or sit down on the earth and relax? Just taking time to take in the natural world with all your senses, in a situation that feels safe, is so very healing to the sensitive nervous system. Do what feels most healing to you, as much as your circumstances permit.

Calming Tool #4: Caffeine Consciousness

Finally, here it is, the thing we all hate to hear: when you have a highly sensitive nervous system, you have to be extra careful of caffeine.

Ugh, I know! And I feel kind of like a hypocrite telling you this, because I'm literally sitting here drinking coffee as I write (it's organic, with adaptogenic mushrooms, if that makes it any better).

Anyway, I get it. I'm not here to suck all the joy out of your life. Coffee is yummy. Most of us don't want to give it up, and I'm not saying you necessarily have to. I'm just saying we should be mindful of how much we ingest and tune into whether our bodies are truly happy with our intake or not.

I've heard many highly sensitive people say they cannot handle caffeine at all. Then there are others (like me) who feel very little effect, yet crave it anyway. But have you ever thought about what it is actually doing to your body? How does that magic bean water do its thing?

Dr. Mark Hyman explains it very clearly in a blog on his website entitled, "Ten Reasons to Quit Your Coffee!" (sorry, he said it not me): "The caffeine in coffee increases catecholamines, your stress hormones. The stress response elicits cortisol and increases insulin. Insulin increases inflammation and this makes you feel lousy."[2]

Basically, when we consume caffeine, that little jolt of energy is a result of the body's stress response. For a healthy, strong person with an average nervous system, this may be no big deal—but if you're in the highly sensitive, chronically burnt out, and fight/flight/freeze triggered club, how much more stress response do you really need?

Only you can answer that question.

If someone would have to pry the black magic beans from your cold, dead hands, maybe you could at least try some green tea instead, which contains beneficial antioxidants and just a small amount of caffeine. Hey, don't shoot the messenger. Dr. Hyman's orders.

OK, note from me about six months after I originally wrote this. I decided to stop being a hypocrite and tried giving up coffee, mostly because I realized my pretty severe adrenal fatigue was not going to improve unless I kicked the habit.

I started drinking Mud Water (yes, it's a thing and doesn't involve actual mud) or matcha green tea instead. Guys, I feel so much stronger. There is life beyond the black magic bean water! Just offering a ray of hope to those on the fence.

Calming Tool #5: Get Proper Help When Needed

Sometimes we all need help. Especially if you're an HSP with a history of trauma, you may need some assistance in figuring out how to calm your nervous system. This doesn't mean there is anything wrong with you. Your nervous system responses make sense, but sometimes we get stuck in those protective fight/flight/freeze responses and need assistance getting unstuck.

Fortunately there is help! You may want to look for a practitioner trained in somatic experiencing ("somatic" meaning in the body. This type of practitioner addresses trauma that is stored in the body). Irene Lyon is an expert in this field, and her YouTube videos and online programs are an amazing resource. Go subscribe to her channel or newsletter now. I'll wait.

What We Really Need

So, there you have it—a few simple ways to nurture your nervous system: conscious breathing, gentle movement, immersion in nature, minding your caffeine intake, and getting the proper help when needed.

Easy, right? And yet, admittedly, many of us struggle to follow through with doing these things regularly. Especially when our bodies are out of balance, we tend to crave things that are not so good for our nervous systems. Ironically, we often know what we need, but we'd rather do anything but!

Remember the "sensation seeking" we talked about in the last chapter? Activities that give us little adrenaline rushes or sugary foods that give a spike of energy can be so appealing when we're feeling run down. Plus, when we're desperate to feel better, it's hard to think a lot about what we're doing. At times like this, we're simply in survival mode and doing what we can to get by.

Give yourself a little grace. Remember, healing isn't a linear process and it doesn't happen overnight. As you work on bringing your nervous system into balance, it might help to make a list of your favorite healing activities to refer to when you're itching for something to perk you up. We'll call this a "What Do I Really Need?" list, and it will be a little menu you can mindfully choose from when you know you need *something*, instead of reaching straight for your phone or heading to the snack cupboard. For example you might really need to get out your thoughts and feelings out by journaling. Or you may need to go for a walk or turn on some upbeat music. You might really just need a nap. I'll give you some ideas and you'll add your own based on what refreshes you the most. It makes for a fun and easy self-care practice—you'll find a copy in the journal.

Next up, we're going to talk about more things we can do to care for ourselves and avoid unnecessary stress on our sensitive nervous systems. Hint—it involves one tiny but very powerful word: N-O.

---

1. "It's True: The Sound of Nature Helps Us Relax." ScienceDaily, ScienceDaily, 30 Mar. 2017, https://www.sciencedaily.com/releases/2017/03/170330132354.htm.
2. Hyman, Mark. "Ten Reasons to Quit Your Coffee!" Dr. Mark Hyman, 25 Nov. 2019, https://drhyman.com/blog/2012/06/13/ten-reasons-to-quit-your-coffee/.

Chapter 10

No and Yes

"She had not known the weight until she felt the freedom." --- Nathaniel Hawthorne, The Scarlet Letter

We hear a lot about self-care nowadays, don't we? It's no wonder. A lot of us are sick and tired of offering ourselves up on the altar of constant productivity. All the rushing around, trying to keep up, chasing some illusive something—it's exhausting.

When we inevitably hit that brick wall of burnout, we usually realize we need a little more care. But how? Is it as simple as more bubble baths and me-time? Well, I'm all for some me-time, y'all, but for now, we're going to talk about one of the most basic forms of self-care: *saying "yes" to yourself.*

Of course, in order to say "yes" to ourselves, we also have to selectively say "no" to other things and/or people. Every day, we are inundated with outside options and requests for our time, resources, and attention. If we don't ever say "no," how will we have anything left for our own needs?

In other words, in order to care for ourselves, we need to learn good boundaries—and this can be oh-so-challenging for HSPs (and especially empaths).

Boundaries are the invisible barriers between oneself and what is other than oneself. They keep us safe and protected, and allow us to recognize when something or someone is stepping too far into our emotional or physical space. For a simple example, we might have an agreement with our significant other that we not interrupt when the other is reading.

This can be challenging because, as highly sensitive people, we seem to lack a filter between us and the world. When we absorb so much from *outside* ourselves, it can be hard to differentiate between what is ours and what isn't. The more empathic you are, the more you understand how difficult this is.

As you likely know from experience (and the empath chapter), feeling others' negative energy can cause empaths physical pain. This can make us very desperate to keep people happy, often at our own expense. If this is a struggle for you, remember to be patient with yourself as you explore new ways of being and doing.

We're going to go over a few things highly sensitive people need to say "no" to, and then some things we need to say "yes" to. Some of these topics we'll either have touched on, or will go deeper into in other parts of the book. Trust that I'm not just being repetitive for the sake of it or trying to bore you to tears—right now, we're just seeing how these things look through the lens of self-care.

Why is all this "self-care" and "boundaries" stuff important, anyway? Well, we know keeping our nervous systems regulated is pivotal to overall well-being. When we feel safe and calm, our parasympathetic nervous system can do its thing and facilitate healing.

On the other hand, when we're stuck in fight/flight/or freeze, our health suffers and we're a mess (been there).

A lack of boundaries, including the inability to say "yes" and "no" at the proper times, invites this chaos into our lives. We don't feel safe with others, as their strong emotions carry too much influence over us. And we don't trust ourselves to make good decisions.

The result is: our nervous systems can't catch a break.

Just think of a small child who feels safe and protected by a strong, loving parent. That child's mother or father sets boundaries to make sure nothing will harm them. These include rules for the child (like stay away from the hot stove, or you need to hold my hand at the store). And also, boundaries that keep outside dangers at bay (such as I need to meet your friend's parents before you can go to their house). Perhaps you remember feeling protected like that, or perhaps not. Either way, right now, we have an opportunity to really care for and protect ourselves by setting healthy boundaries.

This can be challenging, because what we learn as children often becomes a pattern repeated throughout our lives. We always look to recreate the familiar, even if the familiar is not so great. If your nervous system was wired for chaos, you may find yourself recreating feelings of anxiety, overwhelm, or conflict—perhaps with the circumstances to match.

Once again, give yourself some grace. You're very human and your reactions make sense. All along, your body/mind has been trying to protect you. But now you have the option to learn new ways to feel safe and protected.

As we go through the things to say no and yes to, imagine how it would feel to become your own loving, dependable, and dedicated caregiver. Wouldn't it be calming to know that if something isn't good for our little selves, we can give it a firm "*no?*"

When we consistently say "no" to things that put us in harm's way and "yes" to things that help us, a funny thing happens: *we start to trust ourselves.* As we develop confidence that we will stay present, step up, and meet our own needs, our nervous systems can finally get a taste of the warmth and safety they have craved all along.

So let's jump in.

Things to say NO to:

#1 Overthinking:

I'm starting with this one because it's often easier to get used to setting boundaries with ourselves than with others. If not "easier," perhaps it is just a necessary foundation to set before we start tangling with those messy empathic boundaries.

Setting boundaries with our thoughts is really a loving thing to do for ourselves. If we stubbornly refuse to do it, we can become our own worst enemy. Natural medicine leader Dr. Darrell Wolfe (also known as the Doc of Detox) said in one of his YouTube videos, referring to our thoughts, "You are the terrorist."[1] Whoa. How true is that? If we aren't careful, we can terrorize ourselves by letting our minds run amok. We have to set good boundaries with our own thoughts. But how?

It may or may not seem strange to you, but sometimes I like to think of myself as a little kid and imagine how I would talk to tiny me. Even if it seems silly, I suggest you try it. What have you got to lose? Just imagine looking your little self in the eyes and gently saying, "We're not doing this, Love. We're not going to think like this right now. It just isn't good for you." This gentle discipline is a fundamental part of self-care.

Creatives and visionaries in particular tend to spend a lot of time deep in thought—which is great, until it isn't. If we find ourselves constantly ruminating, worrying what others think, or imagining every worst-case scenario, it's a good opportunity to kindly redirect our minds and practice saying "no" to overthinking. This is a good time to use the "cancel" trick from Chapter 7 under "The Emergency Brake".

#2 Bottling Up Emotions:

We talked about dealing with all sticky emotional goo in Chapters 6 and 7, but learning how to handle emotions doesn't come quickly for many of us, because we never learned how. Instead, we learned to hide our feelings and adapt to the moods of others. The result can be that we are so disconnected from our own emotions, half the time we don't even know what we are feeling. All our attention is directed outward, while our own emotional needs are stuffed away.

This disconnected way of being has long-term physical and mental health consequences.

If you tend to bottle up your feelings, keep working on the Five Steps outlined in Chapter 7 for making friends with your thoughts and emotions. If you need more help, look into Dr. Jonice Webb's work on Childhood Emotional Neglect (CEN). You don't have to have experienced physical abuse or neglect to have grown up in a home that wasn't fluent in the language of emotion. It's not necessarily anyone's fault, it's just a blind spot around feelings that gets passed down from generation to generation. The good news is, you can stop the cycle by saying "no" to bottling and stuffing, and instead giving your inner child a safe space to feel through all those messy emotions.

#3 Taking in Negativity and Violence:

With digital media being such a prevalent part of life nowadays, we all need to be mindful of what and how much we take in. This is especially true for highly sensitive and empathic people. As the world seems to be more and more conflicted, what may have once been a relaxing scroll through social media has turned into a stomach churning experience.

Whether it be the time-sucking vortex of Facebook or even a trusted news source, our sensitive nervous systems can come away having absorbed all kinds of vitriol and negative energy. The media often feeds fear and divisiveness, neither of which we want to grow within our spirits. Let's not be naive: garbage in equals garbage out.

On the other side of the coin, we might think we're safe when it comes to fictitious entertainment, but there is so much darkness there too. We can't be blind to what dwelling on violence, misery, and downright evil does to us. Of course, as highly sensitive people, most of us are naturally repulsed by violence. Still, some of us have that tendency toward sensory seeking, where we crave input that really isn't healthy for us.

Of course, only you can make these decisions, but understand that none of us are unaffected by what we feed our mind with. Just like a loving parent sets media boundaries with their children, be willing to assess whether these things are really good for you and say "no" as needed.

#4 Unnecessary Activities:

Well, modern life is rarely boring, is it? There are so many places to go and things to do!

I wrote that pre-Covid. The "things to do" have dwindled a bit, huh? Still, even now, there always seems to be something else you should or could be doing, lest you miss out on all the fun and opportunity. And I know, *doing it all* seems very necessary—until we've taken on too much and are zoned out in an overwhelmed coma, wondering where to even start! Been there myself, more times than I care to admit. We have to remember, as highly sensitive people, the lands of Overstimulation and Overwhelm are not places we want to go.

We also need to have a bit of humility in realizing activities can take more out of us than they do others. Someone with a tougher nervous system might feel energized by something that leaves us feeling drained for the next forty-eight hours. Maybe they're sucking the energy from us. Just kidding, but it feels that way sometimes!

We need more downtime than others, including time alone to process our thoughts. Just because there's open space on your calendar doesn't mean you have free time. Your body and mind may already need that space for rejuvenation.

Your inner child may have a fear of missing out and want to say yes to everything. But as adults, we have a responsibility to consider our sensitive nervous systems and not run ourselves ragged. A parent who is in tune with their child has a pretty good sense of how much they can handle, and recognizes not every child is the same. We can practice tuning into ourselves this way, too.

So what kind of boundaries do you need around activities? Especially for empaths, it may help to give yourself space to really think about an invitation or offer before you say "yes" to it. It's OK to take the pressure off by saying, "Let me get back to you." Remember, you are the gatekeeper of a valuable treasure: your time and energy. Don't let yourself get robbed, OK? It's your job to stand guard and say "no" as needed.

#5 Excess Stuff:

We mentioned this a couple chapters ago, when we talked about anxiety and overwhelm. As sensitive people, we are always taking in more from our surroundings—more stimuli, more energy. Naturally, we need less input to even that out. Whatever we have in our possession gives us input and demands our energy in some way. Therefore, we need to be mindful of how much stuff we surround ourselves with.

We'll be diving deeper into how to deal with the overwhelm caused by excess in Chapter 13, but for now, just start paying attention. What things in your environment might be pulling your energy? How, as a caregiver to yourself can you set some protective boundaries around "stuff?"

Maybe you want to think twice about bringing more stuff into your home, waiting a set amount of time before purchasing something to make sure you really need and want it. Yeah, I know our little selves sometimes want to spend all our allowance on sparkly, fun goodies. It might even make us feel safe to surround ourselves with lots of things. For some of us, shopping gives our nervous systems a little hit of excitement, especially if we know we really shouldn't be doing it.

You know I understand this personally, right? Unfortunately, I also know from experience that things can't really give us the safe feeling we crave. Sometimes we have to reassure our little selves that it's OK. Right now, you have everything you need.

#6 Ignoring Our Inner Voice to Avoid Conflict:

Ah...now we get to the difficult one! How often have you found yourself saying "yes" to something you really wanted to say "no" to? Perhaps even when you knew you *should* say "no." Maybe it felt too difficult to deal with the other person's potential reaction, so you said "yes" anyway.

We might file this under empath problems, but truly, it's a learned emotional pattern. Remember what we learned in Chapter 5: if you tend to lose yourself when around others, you may have picked up the belief that your needs, opinions, or ideas are not very important, or you might have learned to be hyper-tuned into another person in an attempt to stabilize their moods and keep chaos at bay.

We already talked about some methods for coping with these empathic tendencies, but let's look at it from a different perspective for a moment. As children, one of our biggest fears is abandonment. After all, we're completely dependent on our caregivers for survival. To have them disappear on us is terrifying.

Of course, some of us lived through that worse-case scenario. Whether a parent physically disappeared from our lives, passed away, or were present but, for some reason, not dependable, our nervous systems and sense of safety were permanently altered by abandonment. As terrible as that was, it's over now—and yet, we can find ourselves recreating the cycle of abandonment, literally, within ourselves.

When we push our inner self aside every time an outside pressure presents itself, we are quite simply abandoning ourselves. It doesn't feel safe, having a self you can't trust to stay strong and present, does it?

This is a deep dive topic, one that requires a lot of healing work to swim through. But if this resonates with you, it's worth exploring how you can start showing up for yourself and being the reliable, loving caregiver you've always needed and deserved. To start you on this journey, let's talk about some yeses!

Things to say YES to:

#1 Our Own Needs:

Well, hello, Captain Obvious, we meet again! Yes, I know you know this. I also know this. And yet, most of us have been programmed to do the opposite.

The collective mentality says we should sacrifice ourselves for others. It sounds nice in theory, but fails to address this basic truth: *strong, healthy individuals make up strong, healthy communities.*

No one wants to be selfish, of course! We do care for others, and make certain sacrifices to do so. But when we constantly neglect our own needs, it's a lose/lose situation. We drive ourselves to the brink, and then end up saying "yes" in all the wrong ways. We think we are being kind in doing self-indulgent things that numb or buzz the nervous system, but really, we're just hurting ourselves in the long run.

So, could we try something different?

What if we said "yes" to practicing breathing and grounding exercises? To quiet time and space for your creative work? What about "yes" to eating foods that nourish you, or to speaking up for yourself? What if we said "yes" to resting as needed? I know this isn't always possible, but sometimes it's "impossible" because of self-imposed demands, or a lack of saying no. Just imagine how your life would change if you started saying "yes" to all the right things.

Do you feel like that change would be good, or does it sound scary? Sometimes we neglect ourselves because, on a subconscious level, we feel comfortable with our present discomfort. Once again, you've been recreating the reality your nervous system was wired for. The emotional patterns of lack, abandonment, and chaos might be well worn in your brain.

This doesn't mean you're a hopeless case, or that you can't create something different. The first step is becoming aware of what's happening, and perhaps you are doing that right now.

Your needs are important, and you deserve to be well cared for. Everyone does! And of course, when your needs are met, you are empowered to help others, as well. We have to relearn that it is *our responsibility* to care for ourselves by being our own strong and present advocate. No one else is going to do it for you!

#2 Trusting Ourselves:

As highly sensitive people, one of our superpowers is our strong intuition. However, some of us suppress that inner knowing and instead make decisions based on whether we receive outside validation. More often than not, that type of decision making will come back to bite you in the butt. Sure, getting feedback from wise people is a good thing, but taking on the emotional opinions of others can muck up the waters, especially for empaths. Too much outside input can lead to losing track of our own instincts.

This doesn't mean you shouldn't ever take advice. Sometimes bouncing ideas off a parent or trusted friend is the best thing we can do. But remember, you are now your very own responsible adult (even if it doesn't always feel like it). You are the expert on your own life. Deep down, you already know what you need.

So, stop second guessing and ignoring your gut. (Psst... we have an entire chapter on intuition coming up, so for now, just chew on the idea of trusting your instincts as a way to say "yes" to yourself.)

#3 An Abundance Mindset:

Many of us have been wired with a feeling of *lack*. Perhaps you experienced going without necessities in your own life. Maybe your parents fought about money, or maybe you just picked up on the cultural message that resources are scarce and there is never enough to go around, while at the same time being bombarded with the idea we need more, and more, and *more* stuff to be happy.

"Never Enough" can become the theme song playing in the background of our lives. The core feeling that comes with the thought of lacking what we need is *fear*, and as you know by now, fear is not our nervous system's friend.

While you'd think fear of not having enough would drive us to create abundance in our lives, that usually isn't true. It's the old rule of, "What you focus on, you find." When we focus on lack, we create more lack. No matter how hard we work, or how much we actually have, we're stuck in a cycle of feeling like it's never enough.

This pertains to more than money. A scarcity mindset means our brains get stuck in fight or flight, limiting access to our higher thinking processes. This leads to poor decision making and stifled creativity. We might get sucked into addictive, sensory-seeking behaviors in an attempt to escape our anxious thoughts by numbing our nervous systems, or perhaps we will choose to stay in toxic relationships because we can't imagine being "without" certain people.

Being stuck in fear and lack definitely doesn't help us tune into our gifts of sensitivity. Being our true selves feels like a luxury we don't have when we're in survival mode.

At the moment, you may not have everything you *need*, let alone want. As times get tougher, more of us may find our physical and monetary resources have dwindled. Shifting to an abundant mindset might seem like a luxury *you* don't have.

While it's true that shifting your thinking isn't going to magically solve all your problems, it *can* help you regulate your sensitive nervous system to feel calmer in spite of what life is throwing at you. We can start by focusing on what we have, instead of what we don't have.

Gratitude shuts down anxiety. You just can't access both feelings at the same time (I learned that from professor, lecturer, and author Brene Brown), so in times of anxiety, try making a list of everything you're grateful for. Sometimes I just have to tell my impatient and fearful little self, "Right now, in this moment, you have everything you need. Everything you will need in the future is coming your way," over and over again, with some good deep breaths.

By thinking abundantly, we can allow ourselves to feel content with what we have now. Abundant thinking calms our nervous systems, making us feel safe enough to stop chasing the illusion of *more*. And that feels pretty darn good.

#4 Honoring the Nervous System:

As a sensitive person it can sometimes be hard to stay away from things that overwhelm and overstimulate us. You might think we'd naturally avoid these activities, but it isn't always the case. Sometimes we even crave them.

Remember, the mind and body always want to be in balance, and will pull us toward anything that seems familiar. This is true even when the familiar is anything but good for us. Being overstimulated can be addictive in itself. Our nervous systems may begin to crave that little buzz, no matter how terrible it makes us feel.

Personally, I've been guilty of this with social media. When I see something online that irritates or upsets me, my brain goes on a little merry-go-round ride of indignation. My guts get all tied in knots. I swear to myself that I don't want to engage again with this internet nonsense, but a couple hours later, I'm feeling exhausted and just want to zone out and scroll, looking for another "hit" of information to rile my brain up. Ugh.

When we're stuck in these cycles, we often find ourselves taking on too much, doing things we really don't want to do, and/or sabotaging what we *really* want in favor of what we want *right now*. It may seem like the only way to change this is by giving ourselves more big fat nos, but that doesn't always work so well.

Once again, your mind and body only want what they think is best for you. That sensitive nervous system just wants to feel safe and balanced, so when you are craving something that doesn't really benefit you (whether it be an unhealthy relationship, junk food, alcohol, excessive media use, or whatever), it is really just your mind and body telling you something is off balance. *The craving is a message.* That's it.

So, usually we get this message and feel pretty desperate to resolve it immediately. But if we just say "no" to ourselves, the issue of being off balance remains. Sometimes it passes on its own, but other times the imbalance persists and we eventually find ourselves giving in to our cravings.

This really is normal. We *need* to be in balance—but is that one thing we know we shouldn't have really the *only* way to put ourselves back into balance? Is gorging on Facebook's circus of political drama really helping me feel better? Or should I do something else, instead?

Partaking in unhealthy habits is, logically, only perpetuating a cycle of disequilibrium. The good news is, instead of mindlessly grabbing at anything that might temporarily ease discomfort, we can instead learn to find ways to truly honor our nervous systems and bring ourselves into a balanced state of healing.

You see, it's not a matter of just depriving ourselves of what we're craving. Instead, it's about realizing there are other ways to honor the message we've received without inflicting harm in the process. You learned some tricks for this in the last chapter. In times of craving, grab the "What Do I Really Need List" from the journal and show some love to that sensitive nervous system of yours!

#5 Growing Ourselves:

Learning about high sensitivity isn't going to do you a bit of good if you: a) view it as some sort of disease, b) use it as an excuse for all your emotional triggers, or c) say, "Well, I am the way I am, and I can't change—because I'm *sensitive*."

Nope, nope, and nope.

As you know by now, being highly sensitive is a gift. It's part of who we are, and it gives us specific strengths as well as struggles. This doesn't mean we can't learn, grow, heal, and gain wisdom. In fact, whether we have a sensitive nervous system or not, we *all* need to work on personal growth.

Notice how I said "work." It doesn't happen automatically. Bestselling author and speaker John Maxwell said it best, *"Maturity does not always come with age; sometimes age comes alone."*[2]

Haven't we all seen grown adults who completely lack self-awareness and emotional maturity? It's sad to see, and sometimes downright toxic to engage with them. Let's just not be those people ourselves, OK? We never want to willfully paint ourselves into a corner with labels, insisting on sitting there until we rot.

Honestly, I have a lot of compassion for those who have spent years and years being "stuck." Lord knows I have felt stuck too. On some level, we are all just little kids, trying to unravel ourselves from generational and societal trauma and just figure out life. We all have some inner wounds.

Wherever and however you feel stuck, don't give up on yourself. Keep reading things that help you understand yourself better, yes, but don't just take in the information. *Do the work*. Practice the journaling prompts and exercises. Make time to hone your gifts of sensitivity. Get help when needed. Be willing to invest time, energy, and money in the things that build you up. You're worth it, one hundred percent. Say "yes" to growth, and you will grow.

#6 Loving Our True Selves:

When you're highly sensitive and empathic, it's easy to lose yourself. I've often found myself physically and mentally weakened by overstimulation and felt overwhelmed because of my and others' energies, wants, opinions—it can all get very heavy. Sometimes it seems like a decent solution to sacrifice our needs and who we are to keep those around us happy.

This can happen without us even realizing it. Remember mirroring? Empaths can get sucked into matching other people's moods without even trying. More consciously, we can also choose to filter ourselves when we fear other people can't handle our intensity. But how do we stop the cycle and truly embody who we really are?

The answer is simple: *you have to really love yourself.*

When you love yourself, you value yourself. There is no longer the need to hide (or to show off and prove your worth, for that matter). You just do what you need to do, feeling comfortably wrapped in the safety of knowing *you are enough.*

Ironically, in this emotionally stunted world, people often act like it's wrong and selfish to love yourself. It's not. Look, if you don't love and accept yourself for who you really are, you probably don't love or accept anyone else in a very healthy way, either. Someone who is full of hate, fear, and self-loathing doesn't exactly radiate love to others. The harsh inner critic is just as quick to lash out at others as it is to berate you.

Sure, we can go all codependent and try to manipulate people into loving us because of our kind actions (because we don't really believe we are lovable on our own). But that isn't healthy for anyone involved, is it? True love for oneself creates more love to share with others. Newsflash: love isn't a limited resource!

A healthy love for oneself also is not self-centered. People who have a humble but loving acceptance of their own shortcomings can pass that compassion onto the other people in their lives. What we value in ourselves we value in others, too. Appreciate who you are, and you will have more appreciation for others. When you know you are enough, instead of comparing and feeling jealous of where others shine, you can celebrate who they are without feeling threatened.

Another fun fact about loving yourself is that it isn't self-indulgent. As we just discussed, love for ourselves involves setting boundaries and saying "no" to ourselves as needed. When we love ourselves fully, we know we deserve good things in life. We will set ourselves up for success in every way.

And yes, dear friend, you deserve this love and care. You deserve it *so* much. I know it probably won't happen overnight, but I hope this book will help you see your worth and start to embrace fully loving and being your true self.

Wow, that was a lot of yeses and nos, wasn't it? But hey, don't get overwhelmed! Keep in mind that it's all up to you. Which yeses and nos do *you* want to work on?

Just pick one or two that resonate and write them down now. Grab that journal and write down whatever is coming up for you when you think about setting boundaries and being your own loving caregiver.

This maybe wasn't the most fun chapter to read. It wasn't too fun to write, either. There's a lot packed into these five-thousand-some words! But caring for ourselves isn't always about having fun in the moment—it's about doing what's most beneficial for the long term, even if it's hard and uncomfortable right now.

Why? *Because you are cared for and loved.*

But maybe we need a little break from talking about ourselves. Hey, I have an idea: let's talk about other people, and how much of a pain they are!

Just kidding. Sort of...

The "people problems" chapter is next.

1. "Show - Doc of Detox: The Official Website of Dr. Darrell Wolfe." Doc of Detox | The Official Website of Dr. Darrell Wolfe. Accessed November 1, 2021. https://www.docofdetox.com/show-1.
2. John C. Maxwell (2010). "Everyone Communicates, Few Connect: What the Most Effective People Do Differently", p.31, Thomas Nelson Inc

Chapter 11
People Problems

"How people treat you is their karma; how you react is yours." --- Wayne Dyer

Finally we get to it! The people problems chapter. Thank goodness—after all, other people are the source of most of our problems, right?

Just kidding...although sometimes it feels that way, doesn't it?

While HSPs and empaths do have some specific people-related struggles, we're not here to blame "others" for our problems.

The reason I waited until the eleventh chapter to talk about our people issues is because once you've done your own healing and gotten comfortable with liking who *you* are, a lot of people-related problems melt away on their own.

Of course, accepting yourself doesn't instantly fix everything, but once you start feeling good about who you are and excited about your life, negative people tend to drop out of it—or, even better, they are inspired to rise along with you. When people are behaving badly, your good boundaries and strong sense of self will allow you to observe without getting sucked into the fray.

Sounds weird, but just wait. You'll see.

Still, I've noticed a few "people traps" we sensitives tend to get caught up in. And when I say "I've noticed," I mostly mean "I've learned about them the hard way."

If we aren't careful, these traps can really keep us stuck. They can prevent us from fully using our gifts of sensitivity. The good news is, we aren't powerless and can do a lot to free ourselves from them.

So, let's dive into four specific people problems we may get tangled in, and discuss how we can cut ourselves loose.

Before we start, however, I have one disclaimer I'd like to get out of the way. By now, you know how much I like to organize things into neat little bullet points, but the truth is, no problem exists in a vacuum. As you'll see, all four issues really are intertwined. But for the sake of making my jumble of thoughts halfway understandable, we're making a list. First up is...

People Problem #1: People Pleasing

Well, you saw this one coming, didn't you? Especially as empaths, we really just want everyone to be happy! I like to think that's because we care very much about our fellow humans, but let's face it: it's also because other people's bad moods can be hard on us. The more empathic you are, the more painful it is to weather someone else's stormy energy, and therefore the more empathetic you are, the more incentive you have to make everyone around you happy.

It's part of human instinct to crave acceptance from the tribe. When we feel someone is unhappy, and especially if we sense they're unhappy *with us*, often our impulse is to abruptly change course and do whatever it takes to cheer them up. Our minds tell us (subconsciously) that this is *the* way to maintain love, safety, and belonging.

While of course we want to be considerate of others, this is a pretty slippery slope.

When we're busy trying to please everyone else, it's easy to lose touch with our true selves. We may end up in careers and life situations we aren't cut out for, make poor decisions because we ignored our gut instincts, or spread ourselves too thin because we can't say "no." Sometimes the consequence is us becoming miserable and resentful, and ultimately losing the respect of the people we so wanted to please.

But how can we stop caring so much about what people think? How can we stop jumping through hoops to our own detriment?

Well, remember when we talked about *purposeful detachment* in Chapter 5? If you're a kind-hearted HSP struggling with people pleasing, this practice is your best friend. When you pick up someone else's negative feelings, visualize yourself literally handing them back.

"Hey, look what I found! I think this is yours!"

Then, imagine yourself stepping away. If you've found something that does not belong to you, why would you do anything else?

We might think we're doing others a favor by carrying their emotions around while doing a song and dance to keep them happy, but guess what? *We aren't doing it for them.*

Nope, not really. We are usually doing it to keep *ourselves* safe from feeling their negative feelings, or from what we imagine would be the repercussions of their unhappiness. But they have every right to feel what they want to feel, and we have every right to step back and let them take the time they need to process things, without us running interference. Really, it is a kind thing to let people have their own emotions at their own pace.

This practice of letting others own their feelings is incredibly freeing—and it's also easier said than done. Detaching from all the empathic emotional goo takes practice and mental discipline. If you feel like, "Ugh, I want to detach but these feelings are sticking to me," that's normal. Keep trying. The more you can catch what's going on, pause, and purposefully pull yourself away from the goo, the easier it will get. I'm not saying you'll ever be completely goo-free, but you'll be much better off than when you weren't conscious of your empathic tendencies.

Other people aren't always going to appreciate you letting them own their feelings. This is especially the case if you've always jumped whenever their emotional display cued you to. They may be none too happy with your sudden lack of response. In fact, they may run smack into your new boundaries and freak out that you had the nerve to put them up.

Leave them up anyway.

If this whole "purposeful detachment" thing sounds a bit harsh to you, remember this: your responsibility when interacting with people is to be kind, honest, and true to your word. It is not your responsibility to be perfect or to keep everyone happy.

What are your thoughts when reading this statement?: "It is not my responsibility to be perfect or keep everyone happy."

Is there a little voice that pops up? Maybe it is saying, "Not true. I do have to be perfect. It is my responsibility!"

This is a place where we sometimes need to do deep emotional work. The belief that it really is our job to keep everyone happy with our own perfect behavior can be deeply etched into our consciousness.

In some ways, it's normal. It is a good and natural thing to want our families to be happy, but the problem comes when we think we can only obtain happiness and safety by sacrificing who we really are and living under a mask of perfection.

These are unhealthy beliefs that we usually picked up early in life through interaction with people who were unhealthy themselves. You are allowed to be yourself, make mistakes, have others disagree with you, and still be worthy of love and belonging. You are allowed all these, even though sometimes this involves others being upset or disappointed with your choices. Such is the icky sticky goo of life.

It's easy to say, "Forget about them, who cares?" when you aren't in the moment, but when it comes down to it, we often have so much baggage weighing us down at the thought of being *disappointing*. I've felt it too.

What happens when you hear the words, "I'm so disappointed in you?"

Does your gut kind of drop, like mine does? This phrase is so heavy, and makes us feel so unsafe. It's like a warning is being put out: the tribe has spoken, and you are in danger of being rejected.

When you think about it, what does "disappointed" really mean? I looked it up, because I'm nerdy like that. According to Merriam-Webster, the definition of disappointed is: *defeated in expectation or hope.*[1]

Of course we all have hopes and expectations around our relationships. For example, I hope my children will make good choices as they grow so they'll be happy. I also expect them to do certain chores. Say it's my son's turn to do the dishes. When I wake up and find my favorite coffee mug still in the sink, I'm going to be a bit disappointed that my expectations weren't met. I'll ask him, "Dude, what happened to washing the dishes?" And no doubt he'll have a really impressive excuse, like that his brother was supposed to do it.

While these types of interactions are normal, saying "I'm so disappointed in you" takes it to a whole different level. It's like saying "You didn't do what I wanted you to and now you have made me feel defeated and depressed." It carries the tone of victimhood, framing the other person as the disappointing perpetrator. Usually it's said as a way to shame and manipulate.

It's true that sometimes we forget to do our chores or fail to meet an obligation, and we end up disappointing someone. We should own up to that and apologize. But if someone's hopes for you go beyond expecting you to be kind, honest, and keep your agreements, are they really being reasonable? Or are they overstepping boundaries?

Even as parents, we can't predict who our children will grow up to be. We just have to guide and support them as they figure out their own path. Although you may worry about disappointing your own parents or loved ones, be wary of being manipulated into abandoning your own hopes and dreams. It's not really anyone else's job to set expectations for your life. Besides, if you are doing all those core things that give you strength of character, are most people really sitting around depressed and discouraged because you are who you are? Probably not.

If someone really does want to sit around and pout because you didn't make their hopes and dreams come true, hand their feelings back to them and step away.

What people might describe as their "disappointment" in you, usually has very little to do with *you*. It actually has everything to do with *them* projecting their expectations and inner worlds onto you.

Guys, people do this a lot. We all have a tendency to protect our egos by imagining our own faults in other people. As one of my favorite anonymous memes said, "if you knew how much people function by projecting, you would learn to take nothing personally." Truly understanding *why* we shouldn't take things personally is a huge milestone.

But again, sometimes we really do mess up and disappoint our loved ones. Sometimes we just can't (or choose not to) do what they expect. And when that's the case, they have every right to feel their feelings about us.

It really isn't right for us to rush them through their emotions, or even (gulp) try to manipulate the situation in our favor. It hurts sometimes, I know, but we have to give our people space to feel what they need to feel.

Let's consider another angle: when we get stuck in people pleasing mode, usually we are simply focusing too much on *ourselves*. Now that's a mind bender, isn't it? Let me explain. When we're worried about what others think, what are the thoughts going through our heads? Perhaps we think, "If I speak up, they won't like me," or "If I do what I want to do, they'll think badly of me." Maybe we're working on our passion project and imagine others snickering about us saying, "Who does he (or she) think he (or she) is?"

The funny thing is, these musings aren't reflecting a concern for others, are they? We're just imagining how their perception might make *us* feel rejected. Instead of focusing on how what we feel called to do might benefit someone else, we're focused on keeping ourselves safe.

Which, once again, is normal. Your nervous system just wants to feel safe, but that sense of safety we get by hiding our gifts under a rock is an illusion. It doesn't make us safe, and it doesn't help anyone else.

Remember, someone needs you to share your gifts of sensitivity. Instead of getting stuck on how the haters will mumble about you, think of who you can help just by being who you were meant to be.

The truth is, other people are probably not thinking of you at all! They are also too busy worrying about what people think of *them*. Right?

When you are grounded in purpose, it transcends the what-do-people-think mentality. What they think just doesn't matter anymore. Purpose is an unstoppable force. There is no way you can not do what you are supposed to do when you are guided by purpose!

And guess what? You had a purpose long before anyone had an opinion. No one says on their deathbed, "I really wish I had been less of myself, kept quiet on things that mattered, done more things I didn't want to do, and kept my haters happy."

No one says any of that, and neither will you. Live your life.

People Problem #2: Attracting the Wrong People

The second struggle HSPs and empaths often have with people is that they are simply surrounded by the wrong ones!

A long while back, I saw a post in a group for highly sensitive people. The poster had been chatting with a guy she met on a dating site, and he had ended up saying some really awful and completely inappropriate things to her. I can't actually remember what it was, nor would I want to share any identifying details of this story, but think "red flags all over the place, drop this one like a hot potato and *run*."

I believe her purpose in posting was just to vent. She wasn't planning on sticking around to see what happened next, and just seemed shaken by the whole interaction. But it was the comments that shocked me. A lot of those who chimed in didn't feel sorry for the poster—they felt sorry for Mr. Creepy! Many responses were along the lines of, "I can't believe you're being so mean to him. How would you feel if someone just blocked you after talking to them for two days?" and, "Think of how he feels. He's probably a wounded HSP!"

Huh?!

This is exactly how highly sensitive and empathic people get themselves entangled with the wrong folks. Projection.

Imagining that because you are a kind person at heart, everyone is a kind person at heart, is a dangerous game. Maybe even online-creepy-dude-or-gal (who has become "so attached" to you over a whole 48 hours) really is wonderful deep down inside, but no matter how wonderful, if a person has let their demons take over, they can wreck your life just the same.

To stop projecting and protect ourselves, we have to step out of our emotional responses and face facts. Not everyone cares as much about your well-being as you do about theirs. Not everyone has good intentions.

Yes, everyone has wounds, but that does not mean you should invite everyone's pain into your life.

Another reason we surround ourselves with the wrong people is simply because we aren't sure what's normal to put up with. If you grew up in a dysfunctional family, toxic behavior may seem ordinary and expected. You may have protected yourself by going along with things you shouldn't have had to put up with.

When you have a history of being treated badly, it's hard to figure out what a healthy relationship looks and feels like. In fact, since our brains were wired for chaos and disconnection, we may feel *more* comfortable with people who help us repeat the patterns we're used to. Stepping out of ourselves and attending to a volatile person's whims might make us feel right at home.

You see, if our first human interactions were not healthy, it affected how our nervous systems were wired. Since our nervous systems only know what they've experienced, it isn't just a matter of *logically* knowing we should be treated well; it will take conscious work to develop patterns of healthy connection. Unfortunately, many of us go through life having no idea we need to do this work.

Before we can attract the right people, the ones who are capable of having healthy relationships with us, we have to get comfortable setting boundaries. We have to become our own loving caregiver, so we will stick with ourselves no matter the mood of another person. When you have a healthy relationship with yourself, it fosters a necessary sense of self-preservation that prevents you from dragging home wounded tigers. No matter how sorry you feel for them.

And by the way, while we shouldn't get tied up with toxic people, I *don't* mean we should drop a person like a hot potato anytime they irritate us. To have good relationships, we have to be willing to forgive others, and they have to be forgiving of us, as well.

After all, there are no perfect people. If we don't want to be hermits (or only want to be hermits some of the time), we're going to have to put up with some quirks.

Really, it's a gift to be able to look past people's foibles and see their inner beauty and potential—and as empaths, we've got this ability in spades. We don't just see people on the surface; we see them multi-dimensionally. The bad news is, we can tint our 4D rose-colored glasses too much for our own good.

Remember how we talked about projecting? People tend to project their own inner experiences onto others. We usually think of this in the context of the negative.

For example, maybe someone has a tendency toward jealousy. Without acknowledging this in themselves, when triggered by another, they just assume the person is jealous, because that is how they would respond.

We all make our own little assumptions, don't we? We tend to automatically conclude that others think and feel just like we do. Except often, they don't.

If we've learned anything so far, it's that HSPs have a pretty different experience in the world than most. Every individual has their own unique history and biology shaping their viewpoint and reactions. You never really know what is going on inside someone else's body and mind, yet our first instinct is to assume the other person's inner world mirrors ours.

But you know what's so much easier than working on overcoming projection? To focus on fixing others instead of ourselves!

Yes, that was a joke. But it's also painfully true, and therefore is our next people problem.

People Problem #3: Fixing and Rescuing

Are you feeling pretty insistent on bandaging up a wounded tiger? I know. Poor big kitty. But bear with me as we hash out why it is often kinder to let wounded humans do their own rescuing.

First, why is fixing and rescuing sometimes a problem for sensitive and empathic people?

Well, it isn't a problem to want to help, right? And if you have some of the healer type in you, it's literally who you are. You're a born helper. You have deep empathy for others and feel moved to assist them whenever possible. That's not a problem, it's a gift. However, it can *become* a problem when we cross a fine line.

Remember, the healer archetype can't actually heal people. They can help another feel safe and supported, which is conducive to healing, but even an expert in healing is still just a guide for another person. When it comes down to it, *humans have to heal themselves.* You can't force them into it. They have to want it, and they have to be ready.

When people aren't ready to heal, or are just in the middle of working through things, they struggle. And it's hard to watch, isn't it? As empaths, it can literally hurt!

Sometimes it *seems* quite obvious from the outside that a person is causing themselves a lot of pain. We imagine we know their story (even though we probably don't). We think, *oh man, I can help them turn this around and things will get so much better for them.* Perhaps we imagine they just need a friend to guide them. It sounds promising enough, doesn't it?

So we try to give them some guidance, and they love us for it, at least at first. After all, we're the ones who will listen to their rants. We're the first to message after they share some vague (cough, attention seeking) post on social media. They can't help but enjoy having someone pay attention to them, and as we know, empaths pay attention like no one else.

Our struggling person gets used to coming to us for advice, and we're always happy to give it. It feels good to be needed, doesn't it? But after a while we start to get frustrated.

Why do they never follow through on my suggestions?
They keep going through the same vicious cycles!

If only they would just listen to me!

The person keeps having more problems and we keep giving more advice. Sooner or later, we notice they get a little cold toward us. They don't want to share their struggles anymore, and frankly we don't want to hear it.

At the same time we wonder why we aren't appreciated when we're just trying to help. Isn't that what a good friend does?

Well, not necessarily. It can come as an unpleasant surprise that people rarely want advice.

I really thought for a long time that when people complained about their problems, they were asking for ideas (AKA solutions).

Oops. That was wrong.

Guess what? Advice is almost never helpful. Unless they are asking something useful like, "What is that clunking sound in my car?" or, "How do I grow zucchini from seed?" and you happen to be an expert on that thing. Then by all means, advise away!

But giving advice on life? Nope.

People are the experts on their own lives. Believe it or not, they already know the solutions to their problems. Even if they say they don't, on some level, they do.

If someone's life isn't in alignment with what they say they want, there's a reason. Quite possibly, just like most of us, they struggle with repeating unhealthy patterns and trying to sort out why they do what they do. They may choose what seems wrong and painful to us, from our vantage point, but it isn't our job to figure out their whys and hows.

We have to learn to respect where others are on their journeys and not try to rush them through the hard parts.

What I've noticed most is this: people are usually either where they are supposed to be or where they have chosen to be.

Really, how do we know this thing they are struggling with isn't teaching them an important lesson they need to learn? I know sometimes I would have liked to have been spared a life lesson or two, but looking back, the discomfort prepared me for something else in the long run.

Who are we to decide someone needs to be shoved—er...*helped* along from where they are? Most of the time, it's loving to let them be where they are. If you love them, be willing to sit with them there. Listening and asking how you can best support them is helpful. Trying to redirect their trajectory is not, and will have them resenting you sooner or later.

By the way, I realize all of this is funny because I'm basically giving advice on not giving advice. Man, old habits die hard, don't they?

Of course, occasionally, you find someone who wants your life advice. One more tiny piece of advice from me: *run!*

Being someone's advice guru may sound like a flattering gig. An unpaid gig, but we might find it tempting nonetheless.

Unfortunately, there are those who try to avoid personal responsibility by having someone else decide things for them. Never be that someone else.

When we take the burden of decision away from a person, we're really just stunting their growth and healing. It's like seeing a baby bird hopping on the ground and, bleeding heart that you are, you just have to pick it up and move it to safety. But you didn't realize it was already safe, and by interfering, you may have just done more harm than good.

People and baby birds alike need to build up their strength. It might sometimes look awkward and scary, and we think we can help them circumvent the hard part, but that doesn't do them any favors in the long run.

Along these lines, one of the first things we learned in coaching school is that our job is to view people as capable and hold them accountable. Surprise, our job is not to fix or give advice!

While you aren't your friend's coach, you can still do them a favor by viewing them as a capable human being. Recognize them as the expert on their own experience. When they ask for your advice, it may be more helpful to turn it around and ask them what *they* think they should do. They probably just need to talk out their options and perhaps feel reassured. Or maybe they just need to vent. But either way, they know more about their lives than we ever could.

Besides, do you really want the responsibility of being their decision maker? Heck no.

The situation with a person who constantly needs rescuing with acts of service is similar, but more complicated. Obviously when someone truly needs something, it isn't kind to smugly say they should just rescue themselves. There are real needs and real emergencies, whether or not someone created the problem for themselves.

To make sure we can recognize where the line is between being helpful and enabling bad behavior, we need to work on our own boundaries. Some of us healer types have histories which caused us to develop patterns of codependency. We may feel deeply responsible for others' problems.

Once again, when we get healthier, we'll be able to recognize the warning signs and know when to say no. A healthy healer with strong boundaries will still find plenty of opportunities to be generous and offer support, without being sucked into dangerous or toxic situations.

Thus far, we've mostly talked about fixing or rescuing friends. The tendency toward this dynamic with romantic partners is all the more messy (and dangerous).

Sure, trying to fix and rescue friends can bring a lot of unnecessary stress and drama to your life. But taking on a boyfriend, girlfriend, or spouse as a fixer-upper project? That has to be right at the top of the life-ruining-decisions list.

We all know it's true, but people do it every single day. Why? Well, it's often because we're recreating what we know, or, we just don't know what to look out for before getting emotionally attached.

As the saying goes, love is blind. When you've fallen for someone, it's hard to see the red flags, no matter how furiously they are waving. Highly sensitive people feel things deeply and tend to get sucked in quickly, so it's wise to be aware of both our own weaknesses, and what we need to look out for in a potential special someone.

When it comes to finding the love of their life, people seem to wonder a lot about who they are most compatible with. Perhaps this leads to looking out for the wrong things. One might muse on whether an INFJ personality type is compatible with an ESTP (referring to Myers-Briggs personality theory), or if an HSP should marry someone who is also an HSP.

Well, here's the thing: emotional health is more important than personality or traits. Any personality type can behave badly if they are unhealthy. And none of us are completely healthy! We all have wounds, triggers, and things we need to heal.

So we obviously won't ever find a perfect partner. But some are more likely to recognize their own weak spots and work on them. Others prefer to project blame and lash out when they fall short.

Now, if you don't have good boundaries and tend to want to fix people, which one do you think will find you like a moth to a flame?

Yup, the one who wants someone to blame.

Whereas someone else may call them out on their behavior, the empathic healer type cuts people a *lot* of slack. After all, we are so good at seeing people's potential.

When they behave badly, we realize on some level they're just hurting. In fact, maybe when they lash out, we blame ourselves too. Pretty soon we're walking around on eggshells, shrinking and censoring ourselves in an attempt to keep our wounded tiger in a good mood.

And as much as they enjoy having someone else to blame, they are all too happy to keep us on as a permanent scapegoat. Sound familiar?

Let's dive a little deeper into this with our last sensitive people problem. In fact, this last problem is so important, we're going to give it its own chapter.

---

1. Merriam-Webster.com Dictionary, s.v. "disappointed," accessed November 3, 2021, https://www.merriam-webster.com/dictionary/disappointed.

Chapter 12

The Narcissist Factor

"When someone shows you who they are believe them the first time." --- Maya Angelou

And here it is, our fourth people problem: *the narcissist factor*.

You've probably heard (or had the unfortunate experience of learning the hard way) that empaths attract narcissists.

Not everyone who exhibits bad behavior is a narcissist (and maybe the word gets thrown around a bit too much), but since the empath and the narcissist are an infamous pairing, we're going to talk about this particular problem specifically.

So, what is narcissism, anyway?

Narcissistic Personality Disorder (NPD) is a diagnosis given by psychologists or psychiatrists when people meet certain characteristics. Psychology Today list some hallmarks of NPD as "a grandiose sense of self-importance, a lack of empathy for others, a need for excessive admiration and the belief one is unique and deserving of special treatment."[1]

Going another step, we may find ourselves crossing into the lair of the sociopath. Again, Psychology Today has helped me clarify the concept. "Sociopath" is not a clinical term, but indicates someone who has "a profound lack of conscience".[2] Not feeling bound by natural laws of decency to others, they go through life exploiting and manipulating, perhaps all the while exhibiting a charming exterior.

While I do have firsthand experience with such people, I'm certainly no expert on determining who qualifies for the "narcissist" label and who does not. For our purposes, we aren't going to split hairs too much over terminology. Just as someone doesn't have to be diagnosed with depression to feel depressed, one also does not need to have NPD to act narcissistically. You don't need an official personality disorder diagnosis to determine if you can have a healthy relationship with someone. As we'll get into, your intuition already knows what's up. This chapter is all about you tapping into your resources and learning to protect yourself as needed when you encounter an unhealthy relationship.

Why is this chapter important? Well, nothing will squelch your gifts of sensitivity and put you into nervous system dysregulation quite like living with a narcissist. Even after they are long gone, you may struggle to recover your health and self-worth. The same goes for any children or future children involved.

I know, as I am one of those children myself—and probably many of you are, too. While we can't change the past, we can protect ourselves and our little ones by being careful about who we allow into our lives. But sometimes, our compassion overrides caution.

Being so good at seeing potential, we really may not want to give up on the object of our interest, even if all those red flags are a' wavin'. It's easy for us to empathize, imagine what might have brought him or her to this point, and think our love will heal and save them.

It sure sounds dreamy in our romantic little heads, but unfortunately, that's not how it works. Naturally, people with narcissistic personality disorder are humans, too. That said, while I don't want to say anyone is a hopeless case, the truth is these people rarely change. Not because they couldn't, but because their fatal flaw is that they cannot see any reason to change! After all, in their eyes, everything is someone else's fault.

This quote from Dr. Annie Kaszina sums it up (find her on Instagram, she's a specialist in abuse recovery): "People always ask, 'Can they change?' But the real question is, 'Why would they change when hurting someone who loves them gives the Narcissist exactly what they want?'"[3]

Unfortunately, some people's interest in others is only based on what they can get from them. The narcissist is addicted to feeling special, admired, and important. Since empaths are wonderful at giving reassurance and making people feel good about themselves, we are the perfect supply line for their pathological need.

The narcissist may carefully craft a life that looks perfect from the outside (to gain more admiration), which means you become a literal trophy in their showroom. They will manipulate you into continuing to feed their hungry ego and also blame you for anything that might reflect badly on them, no matter if it's completely their fault! As long as they have someone else to control, take advantage of, and blame, the narcissist has no reason to change themselves.

Narcissist or otherwise, when someone is exhibiting toxic behavior, they need boundaries. They need people to stop putting up with their crap. If you instead choose to take responsibility for caretaking the volatile beast inside of them, you're simply enabling them to continue along a very destructive path. If you really want to help them, the best thing you can do is to not be around to be their scapegoat.

If you're hoping you can fix your narcissist, please realize you have zero power to heal or change another person. As we've discussed, this is a big trap for the empathic healer. We want so much to help, but getting entangled with a narcissist only sucks away all your energy and resources. Not only will you not be able to help them, but you probably won't be able to help anyone else, either. Instead, the power you give them may very well wreck your life—and your children's lives, if you have any.

So please, stop worrying so much about saving people who choose to bask in their own toxicity. Instead, be your own loving, responsible caregiver and protect yourself, first. Trust me, your narcissist will take care of themselves just fine, they always do.

I realize some of you reading this are already living with narcissistic abuse. As I said, I've experienced it too, and I'm so sorry. It's very easy for us to get pulled into these situations, as these people are smooth and will take advantage of our kindness and empathy in every way they can. And once again, sometimes it's all we know, and so we are drawn into the same patterns and experiences we are used to.

It isn't your fault. We have to forgive ourselves for what we didn't know. Once the narcissist has you in, they make sure it's hard to get out. Please seek out help if you are experiencing abuse.

While researching this chapter I came across an anonymous meme that said, "An educated empath is a narcissist's worst nightmare." I think that is true. A narcissist wants to control, and an educated, empowered empath is not someone who is easily manipulated.

Much of what we talk about in this book, (building self-worth, trusting your intuition, etc.), will give you a leg up, here, but most of us don't know much about narcissists until it's too late. And even if we grew up with this type of abuse, we still may not know the warning signs to look for at the beginning of a relationship. And as we've talked about already, people are often magnetically attracted to the familiar, even if the familiar is toxic.

So, I wanted to make you guys a list of warning signs to look out for *before* you are trapped in the narcissist's web. If you're an empath out there in the dating world, I hope it will be helpful.

As you guys know, I'm not a psychologist or an expert on any of this. It just comes from research, observation, and years of soaking up counseling tidbits from Instagram! Use this wisdom to spark your own research and reinforce your intuition.

Warning Sign #1: Being swept off your feet

Narcissists can be charming characters. They know what to say and how to act in order to get what they want. And sometimes, that "thing" they want is *you*.

While most people want to impress a new love interest, the narcissist takes it to the next level. This is known as "love bombing." Instead of taking time to build the relationship, they move way too fast.

The love bomber might spin lines straight out of fairy tales about love-at-first-sight or soulmates. They go over the top with gifts and gestures that border on inappropriate. They might shower you with compliments to the point it almost seems disingenuous (because it is), or perhaps they spring a last-minute, exotic getaway on you (without any regard for your schedule or prior commitments).

And if you say no or attempt to set boundaries? Cue all the anger, sulking, and guilt-tripping.

A little note: the average person who has experienced rejection or abandonment may feel initially hurt by your setting a boundary. They may even sulk a little, because boundaries trigger their wounds. However, they are still going to *respect* it. When it comes down to it, they will be more concerned about your feelings than getting their way. The narcissist, on the other hand, does not respect you or your boundaries and will likely only amp up the pressure.

Warning Sign #2: The relationship feels suffocating and/or intrusive

During the love bombing phase, you may be very flattered by all the attention—but the body always knows when something isn't right. That gut feeling of being uncomfortable and suffocated is a huge warning sign.

The narcissist may want to be with you or have tabs on you all the time. Perhaps they text you constantly or show up uninvited to your home, work, or school. They may say it's because they adore you so much and want to make up for all the years they had to spend without you. In some ways, it may feel good to be wanted...but your intuition knows the truth.

Sometimes the narcissist will pepper you with questions that feel intrusive. Maybe you really don't want to answer, but also don't want to hurt their feelings. After all, they must just really care about you and want to know all about you!

Well, make no mistake: a narcissist will use all this intel against you in the future. This seemingly lovestruck neediness is really just a thinly masked effort to control you. This brings us to...

Warning Sign #3: Loss of control and autonomy

In addition to taking up all your time, the narcissist wants to assimilate you into their perfect little world.

You may find them exerting influence over how you think, act, or dress. They might make you think they know you better than you know yourself. Perhaps they encourage you to give up things you like or want in favor of what they think is best.

This can be tempting to succumb to, because we all want to feel taken care of. And sometimes it can feel like a relief to turn decisions over to someone else. Besides, the narcissist acts like they are doing you a favor in "just being honest."

An example of this might be them telling you that you really aren't good at something you thought you were good at, or that your chosen styles don't suit you. Your intuition will tell you this interaction feels yucky, but your mind may simultaneously say, "But what if they're right? They just want what's best for me."

Remember, you are the world's one and only expert on you. If someone has you questioning all your life decisions and core beliefs, it's a huge red flag.

Warning Sign #4: Isolation

Another thing the narcissist may pressure you to give up for them is your support system. Does the new person in your life not like your friends and family? Are you being given an "it's me or them" ultimatum?

Of course, maybe your friends and family really are awful—I don't know! Still, even if they don't immediately mesh with your loved ones, they should still *respect* your relationships.

If you find your new love interest's dislike of your loved ones peculiar, that's really a red flag. Likewise, if your trusted people are leery of your new love interest, don't be quick to drop them like a hot potato out of loyalty to your new "one and only".

The narcissist will encourage you to cut people off, perhaps waxing poetic about how you are soulmates and you only need each other. Make no mistake, this is because they want you isolated. After all, they need things to look perfect from the outside. The more you are blabbing to others, the less control they have over what you are saying and how it reflects on them.

Also, when you have no one else to talk to, it's easier for the narcissist to control your viewpoint (making you feel like everything is fine, they are perfect, and you are the problem).

Warning Sign #5: Pressure to compromise your values

Sometimes a narcissist will pressure you to lower your standards or do things you feel uncomfortable with. This could involve crossing sexual boundaries, encouraging you to lie or use drugs, or something else. Once again, instead of respecting your boundaries, they will push.

Instead of honoring your autonomy, they want to assimilate you into their way of doing things. And once you've succumbed, they can hold your guilt over your head and use shame to further manipulate you.

Remember too, a lack of conscience and disregard for the rights and feelings of others are the hallmarks of a sociopath. Don't let their otherwise charming persona fool you. If someone is trying to convince you to do things you know are wrong, *run*.

Warning Sign #6: Walking on eggshells

As empathic people, we are experts at detecting changes in people's moods, and often we're prone to adjusting ourselves to soothe them. Well, as you can imagine, the narcissist loves that—and they aren't oblivious to our efforts to keep them happy, either. On the contrary, they'll use our empathic sensitivity to manipulate us.

You may find your narcissist is a very volatile character. Perhaps you can't have an honest conversation with them because you fear their reaction. Maybe they use threats of hurting themselves or others to keep you in line, as if your actions will "make" them lose control.

Remember, a narcissist does not see any fault in themselves. It's always someone else's fault, and they are happy to make you that person to blame. Know that, in reality, you are not responsible for anyone else's bad moods or behavior. A person wanting to blame you for the actions they choose to do is a giant, bright red flag!

Warning Sign #7: Confusion

I think I've heard it said that confusion is the first sign you are dealing with a narcissist. Somehow it ended up last on the list, but I imagine it probably is one of the first things we feel around these types of people.

After all, we want to think the best of others. And on the outside, they likely seem very charming—perhaps even too good to be true. Yet, something inside of us is whispering, "This isn't right."

Again, the intuition, the body, the subconscious mind—whatever you call it—this part of you always knows. It's our conscious mind that tries to make excuses based on social norms, past experience, and what the eyes see. When experiencing confusion in a relationship, it's very important to tap into what your intuition is telling you.

As the relationship with the narcissist goes on, you'll likely find the confusion escalates. This is purposeful—this is the beginning of gaslighting. Gaslighting is when someone makes you feel crazy by denying your reality. Perhaps they tell you something didn't happen as you know it did. They insist you are overreacting, you are crazy, or just "too much" when you get upset. You may indeed start to feel like you're losing your mind. You wonder if it really is just you.

This is again where it's handy for the narcissist to have you isolated from your friends and family. After all, your friends and family would be the ones you'd call for reassurance that you aren't ready for the looney bin. Without anyone else to talk it over with, you're stuck trying to make sense of the narcissist's convoluted version of reality.

So, if you're feeling confused, honor the message of confusion. It means something isn't right. What your mind wants to be true isn't matching up with what your body already knows.

Of course, relationships are messy, and we don't want to jump to the conclusion that everyone who rubs us the wrong way is a narcissist. Any person can mistakenly cross a boundary and make you feel uncomfortable.

Maybe someone legitimately doesn't like one of your friends, isn't a fan of your Hawaiian shirt and Birkenstocks look, or disagrees with you on a topic you both feel strongly about to the point it feels eggshell-y to broach the subject. Sometimes things do move too quickly with romance, and you need to back off a bit. While conflicts like these will always arise, take note of whether the other person respects your thoughts, feelings, and autonomy.

Do they honor your boundaries, or is there always some sort of manipulation (even through gifts or flattery) to try to integrate you into their world, their way? As I've said before, your intuition is already telling you what's up. You already are the expert on your experience. Still, if you aren't sure about whether your relationship is healthy, this is a place where asking for the perspective of trusted people in your life can be valuable. You know what I said in the last chapter about "advice", but another person who isn't emotionally invested may be able to spot and confirm the red flags your mind has tried to gloss over. Another option is to find a therapist who specializes in recognizing abuse.

My hope is that this little section of the book helps some of you avoid a lot of pain. Always remember, your gifts of sensitivity are so needed. Spending your time and energy on toxic people who drain your life force is too great of a sacrifice to make.

And no, it really doesn't help those people, either. They need to continue on their own path, wherever it takes them. We can't change another person, and if we try to do so, we'll likely end up in a world of hurt. As much as we like to see the good in people, there are dangerous people out there who will never change. Our best defense against them is to work on ourselves.

Alright, you can now print off your "Educated Empath" certificate.

Just kidding, there isn't a certificate—and we still have more to learn. I've mentioned "intuition" several times in this chapter, and we're about to dive deeper into that topic. In the next chapter, we'll learn why, as a highly sensitive person, you really should trust your gut.

---

1. "Narcissism." Psychology Today. Sussex Publishers. Accessed November 3, 2021.
https://www.psychologytoday.com/us/basics/narcissism.
2. "Sociopathy." Psychology Today. Sussex Publishers. Accessed November 3, 2021.
https://www.psychologytoday.com/us/basics/sociopathy.
3. Annie Kaszina, October 21, 2021.
https://recoverfromemotionalabuse.com/.

Chapter 13

Trusting Yourself

"Logic merely sanctions the conquests of the intuition." -- Jacques Hadamard, French mathematician

I don't always make the best decisions. I feel quite comfortable telling you that, since we've known each other for a whole thirteen chapters now. I also feel comfortable because I know *you* don't always make the best decisions, either!

After all, no human *always* makes the best choices. We usually are just doing the best we can with the information we have at the time. Sometimes we get so tangled up in emotions and fear that our critter brains take over and we end up acting on impulse, even though logic tells us we'll likely live to regret it.

But you know what? It's OK. This is all part of the human experience. You might think we'd be used to it by now, but sometimes—after having enough lapses in judgment—we start to lose confidence in our own ability to navigate life. We might wonder how we can ever trust ourselves when it seems we're always bungling things up.

Trusting ourselves is tricky. After all, we don't want to trust blindly. We have to acknowledge we have blind spots that sometimes muddle our decision-making abilities. For example, aren't we amazing at talking ourselves into what we want, even if we know in our gut it's a bad idea? Um, yeah, been there and got the T-shirt.

It reminds me of a famous Bible verse: *"The heart is more treacherous than anything else and is desperate. Who can know it?"*[1]

It's true; we can get ourselves into quite a mess when our emotional heart is in the driver's seat.

Still, there is a part of us we need to learn to trust: the part we might tend to override with our heart's wants and fears and people pleasing. If we learn to listen, it won't let us down.

That part, my friends, is our *intuition*.

Remember back to what we learned from Dr. Elaine Aron: one of the main characteristics of the highly sensitive person is *depth of processing*. This depth gives us sharp intuition. Our minds are always taking in information and weaving it together. We often have great pattern recognition and can see how things fit together without even trying. As I've said before, this often leads to us knowing things without knowing quite how we know them.

We each have our own secret sauce with intuition as well. For example, I'm very good at picking up language patterns. When someone is telling me an experience they had but leaving out names (so as not to gossip), I will almost always know who they are talking about without them saying. I hear the other person's voice in my head as the story is told. Lesson: don't vent with an intuitive.

I can also usually match up written words to their writers if I know them or have heard them speak. So yeah, I know if you copy and paste something you didn't write without giving credit. Mmhmm. Didn't think you'd get caught, did you?

None of this means I'm psychic or reading minds. It's just a bizarre and not very useful form of genius. I might have picked something else if I was choosing, but here I am with the gift of language pattern recognition. I like to think I'm making the best of it.

Enough about my weirdness—let's get back to our gifts of sensitivity. The healer, creator, inventor, sage, and especially the visionary all need to tap into intuition to do their work. All of these callings are future-focused in nature, so the foresight and clarity their intuition provides are invaluable.

Of course, we don't know everything, but for many HSPs, intuition is one of our greatest strengths. It's a major ingredient in our secret sauce. Yet, many of us ignore, squelch, and flat out refuse to use it. Why?

Well, let's address the elephant in the room, shall we? Some people are just plain creeped out by the idea of a person being "intuitive." Maybe you're picturing a psychic in a carnival tent, waving her long red fingernails over a crystal ball.

Well, let me be the one to break it to you: "psychic" and "intuitive" are not the same thing. There is no conjuring or any other realm of creepiness involved in being intuitive. It's just a very human brain doing its very human thing.

This is hard for some to wrap their minds around. If people can't see something, they tend to assume it doesn't exist. Well, you can't see how your remote control turns on the TV, and yet somehow it will conjure up Netflix for you at the press of a button. Funny how that works, huh?

How our bodies and minds interact energetically with our environment is not something we usually talk about, so it seems mysterious. We aren't sure how it works, so we make assumptions. Well, let's stop assuming and take some of the mystery out of the equation.

The Science of Being Intuitive

First off, everyone has intuition. It's instinct, and it's hard-wired into our nervous systems. Highly sensitive people just have a little extra. Depth of processing allows us to pick up on subtle changes in our environment. To put it plainly, we notice the little things others don't. Some of us also sense when something is off with another person's energy.

Remember from our chapter on empaths: both the heart and brain produce measurable fields of electromagnetic energy. So unless you are also willing to tell your cardiologist an EKG is new-age woo-woo, you'd better not try to tell me intuition is creepy.

It's very scientific, really. Our minds are able to take the information gleaned from our environment and weave it together with what we already know to quickly form logical conclusions.

Basically, we are the ones whose noticing and feeling help alert everyone else to danger. Intuitives play a big role in keeping the species alive—but it only works if we listen!

I hope thinking about intuition in this way helps you understand it a little better. As people, we generally fear what we don't understand. Honestly, in my younger years, I really did fear my intuition. When I knew something without knowing how I knew it, I was kind of creeped out. I thought, "How did I know that? This is weird. I'm weird! I can't let anyone know about this."

I had no idea there were other people who had such strong instincts. Feeling like a lone weirdo, I hid it and generally ignored it. When making decisions, I gave other people's feelings and opinions priority over my own intuitive knowing.

And guess what? It came back to bite me in the butt. Every time.

Even if you start out thinking intuition is strange, creepy, imaginary, or coincidental, there comes a day when you just can't ignore it anymore. The most hard-headed of us eventually realize intuition is a part of us we should be listening to.

Your intuition is there to keep you and others safe—and many of us have stories of it doing just that. I'll share with you one of mine.

Years ago, I was standing in line at the grocery store, loading my items on the conveyor belt, when the guy behind me started talking to me. I don't remember what he said; it wasn't necessarily anything out of the ordinary. But as soon as he spoke, a chill ran through my entire body.

Before I could even turn around, I clearly sensed danger. I just kind of nodded at him; all the while, my brain was screaming, "Get out of here as fast as you can!"

As I was trying to engage as little as possible while still being polite enough, I felt he was getting more agitated. He kept trying to talk to me, and I kept trying not to talk to him. When it was my turn and I was able to move forward in line, I caught a glimpse of his leg —he was wearing an electronic tether!

You'd better believe I've never hoofed it to the car and out of a parking lot so fast.

The thing about this story is that people only tend to believe my gut instinct was correct because I happened to also get *visual* proof something was off with this dude. Those who poo-poo intuition might wonder if I'm confused about the whole thing, and perhaps I only got scared after I saw the tether and rewrote my memory after the fact.

Nope. I remember the whole thing quite clearly, and believe it or not, I would not automatically be frightened of someone who has had a run-in with the law.

But here's the real question: what if this young, handsome guy wasn't wearing a tether, but was clean cut and sharply dressed? You weren't picturing him being good looking now, were you? Ahem.

So, if he was pleasing enough to the eye, would you ignore the fact his presence made your blood run cold? Think of a scenario where he was on crutches and asked for your help with his groceries. Would you listen to your gut, or ignore it based on what you could see?

If you've watched enough true crime shows, you know prioritizing visual evidence over instinct has cost people their lives, but listening to your gut doesn't always involve potential psychos. Our intuition is always giving us gentle nudges in the right direction, on little and big things.

Still, most of us have absorbed the message that intuition isn't that big of a deal. Shouldn't decisions be based on concrete, tangible evidence? Even if we're kinda-sorta listening to our gut, don't we need to research and prove the theories provided by our intuition?

Well, if your gut is telling you to research, by all means, research. I'm a big researcher myself, if you haven't figured that out yet. Please, don't be pressured into making a decision until you do your due diligence.

But if your gut is telling you to run? You'd sure as heck better run, even if you have visual proof that says "it's fine."

This is something we all need to remember: *energy is evidence.*

Electromagnetic energy is tangible, meaning it is real, physically measurable, and you can feel it. When you get a gut feeling, your body is sending you messages based on its measurements of the surrounding energy. To ignore those messages because of something as changeable as your visual perception is foolish. Viewing our intuition as wise can create a much needed paradigm shift.

We can misinterpret what we see, and we can mistakenly put our trust in the wrong people. But those visceral, gut instincts are based on our bodies' innate wisdom and abilities to sense what we cannot see. This is why intuition doesn't let us down.

Still, even knowing how valuable and spot-on our intuition is, we can get tripped up. Sometimes we end up letting our emotions stomp all over our intuition. Let's go back to our creepy but semi-hot, tether-wearing guy. Let me assure you and my husband, him being good looking was the furthest thing from my mind, but I'm including that factor for our single ladies and gents to mull over.

Let's say Hot Creepy Guy isn't just in line at the grocery store. Maybe he goes to your church, or he's a coworker or your roommate's boyfriend. Let's say he sports an expensive watch instead of an electronic tether. Maybe the hairs on the back of your neck don't stand up in his presence, but something about him makes you feel uncomfortable.

At this point, protecting ourselves isn't as easy as running to the car and speeding off. Our gut feeling still says *get away,* but maybe we can't physically escape. Instead, we have to create boundaries. This might involve speaking up and facing confrontation. For us empaths, this is especially difficult, because we are so attuned to other people's emotions and often feel responsible for them.

Even though Creepy Guy (or Girl) is creeping us out, we can often fall into the trap of being more worried about disturbing anyone else's feelings than we are about protecting ourselves. It feels easier to avoid confronting the situation, so we start to look for visual proof that our instinct is wrong.

I'm just being silly. Everything is fine. He's probably a nice guy. (Or, *she's probably a nice girl.)*

We whack down our gut feelings and find reasons to justify our silence or compliance, all in an effort to appease our emotional compulsion to keep everyone happy.

Only later—usually when it's too late—do we remember what our gut told us in the first place. How many times have we heard people say, "I knew something wasn't right, but..."

Yes, the paths our gut can lead us down can be bumpy, even if they do end up being the right path to take. After all, sometimes our intuition tells us things we don't want to believe.

I recently read an article talking about how intuition is a parent's best tool to combat child sexual abuse. Most parents whose children had been abused reported having a nagging feeling something was "off," but who wants to believe something that seems too horrific to be true?

Often the perpetrators groomed the victims and their parents, pushing their boundaries more and more to see if they would push back. When they did speak up and set boundaries, that tended to make the predator run for the hills. The ones who worried too much about making waves or hurting feelings paid a horrifically high price.

Pushing away our inner knowing can lead to a lifetime of regret.

How about you? If your gut tells you something is off, do you feel empowered to speak up for yourself, or are you paralyzed by fear of people's reactions?

Sometimes we are so afraid to speak up for ourselves. No matter how strongly we feel about a matter, fear tells us our survival depends on keeping quiet and blending in. Friends, I've been there too. It's a trauma response.

If you're terrified of standing up for yourself, it is *not* because you're weak or destined to be a victim. Nope. It's probably just that somewhere along the way, you learned to be the caretaker of a volatile person's emotions. If they weren't happy, you weren't safe, so you learned to prioritize their needs over your own.

At the time, it was probably a very good survival strategy. But if we keep using it once that situation is over, we can get ourselves in a mess of trouble.

Even if you didn't have a specific person who you needed to walk on eggshells around, we all have baggage around *being nice*. Many of us were taught being nice means being quiet and cooperative. Don't make noise, don't speak up if it might upset someone, and especially don't speak up if you might be wrong. And above all, for Pete's sake, don't look crazy.

Well, sometimes listening to our intuition goes against all of that. When that happens, our emotions put on the brakes, screaming, "Um, hey, intuition! Hold up! Don't you know we're in danger of being rejected if we do this?!"

You see guys, our bodies are wired for survival. Your brain just wants to protect you. This leads to the push and pull between intuition and emotion. Part of you thinks staying safe means keeping everyone happy and being accepted by those around you, but that part is dead wrong. Your survival no longer depends on being approved of by the tribe.

Still, the urge to put others' needs ahead of your own can be strong. It's hard to get past that mental wiring. It often seems like the gentle nudge of intuition is so tiny in comparison to the person bellowing their wants right in front of you, doesn't it? So what do we do about it?

First, we have to be aware of what we are doing. If you find yourself looking for something more tangible to prove your instincts wrong, just notice what you're doing. Ask yourself: why don't I want to believe my intuition on this? What might happen if I do follow my gut? What emotion am I experiencing about that?

Hint: it's probably fear.

If you're feeling pressured by others to make a choice that goes against your intuition, it is very tempting to let that fear take over—and as you know, once fight or flight takes over, our chances of making a rational decision are *kaput*.

So allow yourself to step away from the pressure. Especially as empaths, we do not make good choices when other people's thoughts and energies are affecting us. Give yourself some time and space to decide on your own. (Note: I'm not talking about situations with strangers like the guy in the supermarket. Those are instances when you need to act quickly and go with your gut.)

Remember, you can always decide your intuition was wrong and move on, but often you can't undo a decision that went against it.

These simple steps of 1) noticing what's happening with your emotions and 2) stepping back to give yourself space to decide are very powerful.

Exploring what's going on under the surface of our compulsions and taking the pressure off helps us make clear, conscious decisions. Kind of ironic, but making a conscious, rational decision often involves doing what you knew you needed to in the first place!

Remember, intuition isn't always about life or death. Your inner voice is always there. If we learn to listen to it about the little things, we'll be better prepared when something big comes along.

The Art and Science of Being the Crazy One

Still, you may be surrounded by people who aren't as intuitive as you. After all, most people base their reality off only what they can see and put their hands on. Preferring to make decisions based on concrete, visible factors is part of their personality—and you know what? It's OK.

Their way of thinking is also valuable. The sad thing is, these people often don't know how much they need us intuitives. Frankly, if you have one of these people in your life, they may think you're crazy for following your gut and questioning what they view as obvious.

Well, I have some great advice for you: *get used to being the crazy one.*

I realize that's probably not the advice you were hoping for. It wasn't what I was hoping for either, but it has grown on me over the years.

I realized people didn't get me, I grieved it, and I moved on. In the end, I was usually right. Gotta love intuition for getting to say "told you so." Or at least think it. We're much too gracious to rub it in anyone's face. (Usually.)

The point is, so what if they don't understand you? Once again, you are still safe. You don't need to prove what you know to anyone. The energy is the evidence, whether they understand or not. Besides, time will tell.

It reminds me of math class, when the teacher would inevitably say, "You have to show your work!" Believe me, I didn't like it then either.

Those who rely on concrete, one-dimensional logic always want to see "the work." (I use the word "logic" here very loosely, because real logic is never one-dimensional.) The thing is, intuition doesn't always show its work—at least, not right away.

As a society, we have been so conditioned to prioritize black-and-white, "right answer" thinking that we are often terribly uncomfortable with the possibility of being wrong. Of course, when we go with our gut, there is always the chance we will be wrong. Like I said, we aren't psychic. Our intuition gives us a real fighting chance, but we're going to make mistakes in life, one way or another. Why not make peace with the reality of not having all the information yet?

I know, I know. We all like being right, don't we? Saying "told you so" makes those wounded egos feel so nice and puffy, at least for a moment. But we have to learn to let go of the ego and be OK with the fact we don't—and never will—know everything!

You don't have to always be right to be able to trust your ability to feel your intuition, sift through information, and think. Be open to new ideas and ways of looking at things. The universe is full of undiscovered wonders, and the world is riddled with hidden truths. When we look past the "settled science" and multiple choice bubbles, we begin to see infinite possibilities.

The funny thing is, we "crazy intuitives" often end up with more logical, concrete information to back up our inner-knowing than anyone else. That's because instead of squelching our instinct, we let it lead us down the rabbit holes. We do deep research, because strong intuition leads to insatiable curiosity. The intuitive mind can't just accept something as truth because someone else told us so.

Think of the phrase "ring of truth." Truth resonates with a different energy than falsehood, and we can feel it. This means we can't just brush it off when something doesn't sound right, no matter who is saying it. *We have to seek the truth.*

For many HSPs, this seeking is part of our calling. We are drawn to finding it like a moth to a flame. And yes, sometimes the truth hurts. At least, finding it is a very lonely job. Sadly, sometimes finding the truth doesn't change much, because most people prefer the comfort of lies.

Seek it out anyway.

Of course, thinking about what might be true isn't supposed to be so lonely. After all, we're supposed to be able to discuss our thoughts with others. That's how great ideas evolve and get implemented. But we live in a world where those deep discussions have become rare.

Often, people have their egos so attached to having the right answer it becomes paralyzing. They become too afraid to step into the critical thinking process, or they lash out when one of their core beliefs is questioned.

I can't help but think of Jack Nicholson in *A Few Good Men,* screaming, "You want the truth? You can't handle the truth!"

OK, so he was kind of the bad guy. But sometimes, dealing with people who can't handle the truth makes a person want to scream, doesn't it?

It can be so frustrating when no one around you seems to share the same curiosity and passion for truth. It's grief-inducing when you have all kinds of interesting thoughts and no one to talk about them with—or at least, no one who won't write you off as crazy!

But you know what? You really aren't alone. There are many of us who think and feel the same way you do.

If you are a lonely, truth-seeking intuitive, remember what 19th century German philosopher Arthur Schopenhauer said, "All truth passes through three stages: First, it is ridiculed. Second, it is violently opposed. Third, it is accepted as self-evident."

Time will tell, friends, time will tell. But can you see how following your intuition doesn't make you silly or weak-minded? It's actually quite the opposite. It often takes bravery to go with your gut instead of following the status quo.

And in this crazy, upside-down world, ignoring what you've been programmed to do and instead listening to your inner knowing is quite possibly the most intelligent choice you can make.

Your mind and heart are powerful assets. Own them. What your intuition tells you won't always make sense. Listen anyway. At least, be willing to shut out the noise and explore all the options.

Remember, your intuition's primary function is to keep you safe. Let it do its job. And when you feel like the lone crazy person, remember, you truly aren't alone. There are many of us truth-seeking intuitives out here, asking hard questions, diving down rabbit holes, and making waves right along with you.

After all, sometimes what looks crazy is literally the only thing that makes any sense.

I hope this chapter has left you feeling empowered to use your superhero power of intuition more fully. While we've learned a lot already about how to step into our power as highly sensitive people, it isn't always easy to implement these things.

Daily life can feel overwhelming to us. Sometimes we don't feel cut out for society and all that seems to be expected of us. How's a sensitive soul to cope in a world that wasn't made for us? We'll talk about that next.

---

1. "Jeremiah 17:9." Essay. In New World Translation of the Holy Scriptures: Rendered from the Original Languages. Brooklyn, NY: Watchtower Bible and Tract Society of New York, Inc., 2013.

Chapter 14

Socks & Swampmonsters

"The only people for me are the mad ones, the ones who are mad to live, mad to talk, mad to be saved, desirous of everything at the same time, the ones who never yawn or say a commonplace thing, but burn, burn, burn, like fabulous yellow roman candles exploding like spiders across the stars..." --- Jack Kerouac, On the Road

We HSPs and empaths have an intensity to us. Feeling and experiencing life deeply creates a fire within our being, and that's part of our beauty. However being born to be a firework has its challenges. It's sometimes hard to reign in our passionate selves long enough to accomplish the seemingly boring tasks of everyday life. Is this something you struggle with too?

If so, you might feel like you don't fit in with the good people of the world. By "good," I don't necessarily mean nice humans. I'm referring to those mysterious people who never leave dishes in the sink and can always find matching socks. Those who are just "good" at being people.

We're all just doing our best to keep up with life, but being wired differently means we often don't fit the mold. No matter how hard we try, the struggle persists.

We could be right alongside the good people, and yet still, there's a nagging feeling of being on the outside, looking in.

Maybe we're putting on a good show, but it feels like just that... a show. We hope if we move quickly enough, no one will notice all the balls we're dropping. That is what we're talking about in this chapter: the fear of not keeping up or meeting others' expectations.

This has always been a source of shame for me, and maybe it has for you, too. There are several reasons we might struggle with the business of life more than most. Perhaps you've heard of the term "executive function." Some people do have conditions leading to a deficit in executive functioning skills (which include the ability to plan, focus, remember, etc.), but we're not going to be addressing that specifically. I'm not out to pathologize seeming absent-mindedness—a quick Google search can do that just fine.

Instead, we're going to look at how our struggles come into play with our gifts. In the process, we'll be releasing lots of icky-sticky shame—and instead of mentally beating ourselves up over our perceived lack of organization and/or productivity, we're going to look at ways to work with our gifts and still get things done.

Mind you, I didn't say how to get *everything* done. No one can do everything—but we *can* accomplish enough to maintain our lives and not lose our minds in the process.

Maybe this chapter doesn't sound like something you need. After all, some highly sensitive people are naturally good at keeping things simple and organized while avoiding getting overwhelmed. They don't take on more than they can handle and have routines that serve them. They know they are enough. And maybe they can even find clean, matching socks without fishing under the bed. Who knows?

If this is you, feel free to skip to the next chapter. However, if you're feeling like, "Oh my word, I can never do enough. I'm hardly keeping my head above water," you, my friend, are in the right place.

I'll be honest, this is a hard chapter for me to write. Not because I don't have a lot to say, but because it's an area where I feel so alone. I'm picturing pretty much everyone flipping past these pages while thinking, "Mmhmm, that girl's got problems!"

But another part of me says, *What if feeling like we can't keep up is such a huge source of shame, no one feels safe enough to talk about it?*

Back in Chapter 3, we talked about the pressure this world puts on all of us to *produce*. There is a nagging cultural insistence that we should always be doing something important (and looking good doing it). There's also an unspoken list of what qualifies as important, generally including "things which make money" and "things which keep up appearances."

As we absorb this message of constant urgency, it's easy to feel like we don't measure up. We're like our old friend, the elephant everyone wants to be a lion. She's tired, having had a busy day of elephanting, and someone has the nerve to impatiently ask, "Well, what did you kill today?"

"Um, nothing."

"Ugh, you're so lazy. Is it too much to ask for you to chase down a gazelle once in a while?"

Sometimes it feels like no matter how much we do, or how hard we try, it's *just never enough*. If we're spending time on things that are important to us and being true to ourselves, the so-called good people of the world seem to be shaking their heads in disapproval.

At the same time, just doing the basics and keeping up appearances sucks so much energy. It often feels impossible to do everything necessary and work on our gifts, too.

Friend, you really are enough. We're all just trying to function in a world that wasn't made for us. Let's let those dishes soak a little bit longer and instead, wash away some *shame and guilt*.

We're now going to contemplate six reasons why we may struggle to keep up with the business of life, or just other people's expectations. As you do, release yourself from any negative feelings about the whole thing. You've always done the best you could.

6 Reasons Why Sensitive People Struggle To Keep Up:

Reason #1: The Creative's Blind Spot

"Why did God give me this brain if he wanted me to spend all day cleaning, running errands, making phone calls, and filing papers?" — Me

Raise your hand if you've ever stared into a sink full of dirty dishes and sighed. Ah, the endless dishes. What a drag. And paperwork? Ugh. I shudder just thinking of it.

Let's think back on the gifts of sensitivity we talked about in Chapter 4. Remember the healer, creative, inventor, visionary, and sage? All these types have the ability to see and bring things into existence that do not exist in the present.

Sounds kind of wild, but it's totally true. This is your gift! The healer sees the potential inside a person and knows how to draw it out of them. The creative types mold their imaginative vision into something we can all enjoy, using art, music, mechanisms, or words. The visionary types see how past and present events fit together and recognize how to shift course in order to shape a better future.

You see, all of these sensitive archetypes are future focused by nature. As a highly sensitive person, you were made to create, envision, and heal.

To mindlessly kill tasks all day long? Not so much.

You're often busy pondering over the most interesting concepts, which is wonderful, but when one is so deeply engaged in the fascinating and imaginative, it's easy to develop a distaste for the more mundane business of life. We are so focused on *becoming* that attending to present reality can be our blind spot.

That doesn't mean you should feel guilty about it. Everyone has a blind spot. What if no one told you about blind spots when you were a new driver? Well, you probably would have plowed your car into the side of another vehicle. Maybe you did anyway (I came close once myself). But when we learn to regularly check our blind spots, we can get to our destination without incident.

This means the business of life gets attended to, but we are still able to focus on the future road ahead of us. We'll get to how to do that in a few.

Reason #2: Depth of Processing Leads to Overwhelm

Do you ever feel like you thought of everything you have to do, and now you're too tired to do any of it?

HSPs process everything in their environment deeper than most, so having a highly sensitive nervous system means you are dealing with more sensory input than the average person. It may seem silly, but this takes real energy. Depth of processing can lead us to burn out before we've produced much in the way of visible results. Simply put, it's exhausting!

Don't be too hard on yourself, OK? You just don't have the same filter for life that other people do. This does not make you less capable than someone with a stronger filter on their nervous system; it just means you are literally dealing with more, even under the same conditions. Because of this, it's all too easy for our nervous systems to become overstimulated—and overstimulation is a sensitive person's Kryptonite.

When this happens, we feel totally overwhelmed. No longer being able to think straight, we freeze up. It's like being a deer in headlights.

Since we don't know what to do next and our brains are no longer cooperating with us, we have little choice but to shut down and wait for it to pass. Not exactly a formula for high productivity, is it?

We've already talked about how the stress of having a highly sensitive nervous system can wear down the body. If you've been dealing with this for years, living in a perpetual state of fight/flight/or freeze, you may just be *worn out*.

Adrenal fatigue is no joke. It's entirely possible you feel unable to keep up because your body needs time to rest and heal. Be patient with yourself. You aren't lazy; your body has just worked too hard for too long.

Reason #3: Trying to Copy Systems Designed for Someone Else's Brain

"I know I'm not stupid, but sometimes the simplest things sure make me feel stupid." — Me Again

What's the first thing we do when struggling to keep up? Hide under a blanket and cry? Eat chocolate? Believe me, I've been there too.

We may also look for someone who has mastered the thing we are struggling with. We think perhaps if we do what they did, we will get the same results! And so we buy all the books, courses, systems, planners, and containers they advise us to.

When their advice doesn't work for us (and we're rather broke on top of it), cue the tears and stress eating.

There is no shortage of advice on how to be more productive and better organized. Trust me, as an official information junkie, I've probably sifted through most of it. No doubt much is good, sound advice, but what works for one person doesn't work for everyone. Even advice that resonates with most may do little for you, because you aren't most people.

When you think about it, who usually creates systems and advice meant to help people struggling with organization and productivity? People who hate organizing and would rather fly by the seat of their pants? Laid back, Type B people? Almost never.

Instead, it's usually people who are naturally organized telling you how to do life just like them. But it doesn't work, because you are not naturally like them. Frankly, they have no idea how your mind works. They don't know how much time you spend in an inner world no one can see. They don't experience all the extra sensory input you do, and they aren't pulled to spend so much time doing the seemingly unproductive things that give you life.

Here's a little story that I get flack for every time I tell it. A few years ago, everyone seemed to be buzzing about organization expert Marie Kondo and her book, *The Life-Changing Magic of Tidying Up*. Well, I read it, and tried to work the magic. I emptied and purged and agonized over how many pink tank tops can truly "spark joy," in her words. Each one is a slightly different shade of pink—and I really do like pink.

Regardless, decluttering is really the part I can handle. Sure, it's a pain in the butt and keeps me from more interesting tasks, but I can handle the temporary discomfort. The part where she lost me was the *folding*. Every day, there is more laundry to be done, and having three kids, it already seems endless. Why on earth would I want to prolong the agony by making my skivvies into origami?

I gave it the old college try, but, no exaggeration, I felt like my brain was melting. Apparently that makes me weird, because when I say that, all her fans look at me like I'm a swamp monster.

Maybe normal people do love folding their underwear. Maybe it brings them great satisfaction to see all the little colorful pieces of microfiber lined up in their drawers.

It's a lovely idea, really, but as a swamp monster, it's just not my thing. I might say if I had all the money in the world I'd pay someone to turn my laundry into folded art. But you know what? I wouldn't—because I just don't care!

One could argue the calm of not having to dig for the perfect pink tank top would free up brain space. Fair enough. But I have to pick my priorities, and that's OK.

We all have things that are most important to us, and we know what makes us tick. Don't sacrifice who you are to replicate someone else's vision. When you get advice, sift out what works for you and release the rest.

Reason #4: It's Hard to Replicate What We've Never Seen Done

"Every time I try something new, I slip back into recreating what I've always known." — Also Me

Psst—that is normal! Many of our traits are inherited, and most of our behavior is learned.

Dr. Aron talks about the possibility of high sensitivity being inherited, although plenty of us have to squint to see it in our family tree. Either way, if you struggle with organization and structure, there is a good chance you can trace it back to your family of origin.

For example, my husband is super organized and productive. I would be surprised if anyone on the planet is better at planning, keeping things in order, and getting it all done. Microsoft Excel is his love language. He comes by it honestly—from his great aunt, who, legend says, kept *white carpet* in her garage. He also gets it from his parents, who meticulously maintain a three-acre property of beautiful gardens despite health issues. This family knows how to get 'er done.

I, on the other hand, was raised in a family of intellectual but not-very-organized people. They loved reading, tinkering with inventions, and discussing current events. The maintenance of life was kind of a dull afterthought.

Me? Same. Even though my natural personality type tends to be slightly more organized (and I've done a lot of reading on how to get one's act together), I always feel the pull back to the homey comfort of chaos.

There are surely some of you out there who grew up in truly chaotic environments. You may have never seen life done with intention and structure, so no matter how many planners you buy or how much money you drop at The Container Store, you still find yourself sliding back to what you've always known.

Give yourself some grace, OK? Our early programming is very real, and it is powerful. We can learn new things, but in the meantime, don't mentally pummel yourself for what you don't know how to do yet.

Reason #5: The Stories We Tell Ourselves

"The way I am is the way I am." — Imaginary Curmudgeon

Considering reasons one through four, is it any wonder if we're carrying some limiting stories about ourselves and what we are capable of?

Back in Chapter 6, we talked about the power of our thoughts. Along those lines, have you heard of the Law of Focus? This quote from speaker, coach, and author Rod Hairston sums it up:

"What you focus on you find. What you focus on grows. What you focus on seems real. What you focus on you become."[1]

The words floating around in our minds are powerful! If we're focusing on all the things we aren't good at, it certainly doesn't make us get better. That negative focus can actually exacerbate the situation.

When we tell ourselves stories like, "I'm so incompetent. Maybe I'm just lazy. I'll never be good enough," our minds hear the story as direction.

"Oh, we're acting incompetent and lazy? Yes, ma'am! No problem, I'm on it!"

It sounds funny, but it's just how our minds work. Language gives the brain instructions. Think back on your own experience. Does mentally berating yourself usually make you do things better? Even if you feel temporarily motivated to change, do you quickly find yourself slipping back into old ways? That's usually the way it goes.

When we keep telling ourselves how rotten we are at something, it's really hard to make the shift into *not* being rotten. The story we play on repeat is exactly what is keeping us stuck.

Really, we've all been there. Personally, I've carried so much shame about this topic I have even felt bad about myself when I *did* succeed with getting things in order.

Years ago, I discovered Marla Cilley's FlyLady website and implemented her routines. Before there were a bazillion people giving advice online, Marla was pioneering the concept of online community and thought leadership. She shared her systems for eliminating clutter and keeping a house in order. Being that she wasn't born organized either, she really knew how to talk to a swamp monster like me.

At first, I was so excited and proud of myself...until I realized other people didn't share my enthusiasm over new cleaning routines. Understandably so, but guys, I was so easily deflated.

I started to tell myself this story: "Everyone else already knows how to do this. You are so stupid for needing someone to tell you how to keep your house clean! You'll never even be able to keep this up."

And that's how self-sabotage starts. When we tell ourselves the story that we can't do something, our minds are quick to oblige by not doing it.

Of course, it would be pretty easy to stop there. We could keep telling ourselves we just aren't good enough, then turn our struggles into excuses, giving us permission to stay stuck. Sometimes staying stuck feels tempting, but it's really not an option. Remember your gifts. Someone needs what you have to offer.

You might be thinking, "Well, being organized and productive is obviously not my gift! Can't I just go with what I'm good at?"

Yes and no.

Yes, we have to lean into our gifts and not berate ourselves for our weak spots. But no, we can't just ignore our weaknesses—especially when it comes to the business of life. Life doesn't go away by us pretending it isn't there. I wish it did, but alas, the longer we wait, the more overwhelming and out of control things get, like six months of paperwork that will take all day to sort out, or last night's dishes that are now even grosser to deal with.

If we're living in chaos, our options become limited, making us shrink from our gifts as well. So what do we do about it?

First, we have to change the story.

You are enough. Stop apologizing for who you are. You don't fit in the box, and that is more than OK. I don't fit in the box either, and in fact, I don't even know where the box is. I probably either accidentally recycled it or crushed it in a pile at the bottom of my closet. With or without the box, we are still more than OK.

Reason #6: Your Nervous System is Dysregulated

"Huh?" —Average person, confused by what the nervous system has to do with leaving dishes in the sink.

Well, this might seem like a pretty deep excuse for piles of unfiled paperwork, but we're digging into it. Back in Chapter 9, we talked a bit about the autonomic nervous system and how we can get stuck in fight/flight/freeze modes. As owners of highly sensitive nervous systems, keeping balanced is key to maintaining resilience and being able to do the things we want to do.

Nervous system dysregulation may be a factor in struggling to keep up with the business of life because when our nervous systems aren't balanced, our energy can be all over the place. We might have spikes of motivation followed by super-low lows where we crash and burn.

We also may run into a lot of resistance when we try to carry out our plans. This is because the nervous system is always on alert, sending you messages that it might not be safe to proceed. Constantly having to process whether you really should do something, or do it now or later, is exhausting.

Nervous system dysregulation can also lead to us feeling disconnected from our environments and stuck in our heads. When we've been overwhelmed for too long, our systems just can't process anymore, and we stop noticing a lot of what is going on around us. Therefore, you really may not fully see or process the little messes around you—which quickly leads to them becoming big messes!

If you feel you might be struggling because of dysregulation, don't worry. You aren't a lost cause. The body, including the nervous system, was made to heal. You will probably need some help with this (I know I did), but it *can* get better.

So, by now you've figured out I'm not the person to tell you how to organize your closets or file your papers. However, despite my "let's see, I know it's here somewhere" method of functioning, I do have a few tricks up my sleeve.

Hey, if I managed to get this book out of my head and into your hands, my tricks must work (at least a little), right? For those interested in a swamp monster's bag of tricks, you'll find them in the next chapter.

---

1. Hairston, Rod. "Part 1." Essay. In Are You up for the Challenge?: Get What You Want in Your Life Starting Now, Not Someday, 5. Leesburg, VA: Invictus International, 2006.

Chapter 15

Four Tricks

"If a cluttered desk is a sign of a cluttered mind, of what, then, is an empty desk a sign?" --- Laurence J. Peter

OK, guys, here it is. I've curated four tried-and-true methods of getting things done, specifically designed for us sensitive souls and swamp monsters. And I promise to not say "swamp monster" again for the rest of the book, since I'm on the border of overdoing it.

Let's jump right in.

Trick #1: Reframe Abundance

As we talked about for the umpteenth time in the last chapter, the highly sensitive mind is easily overstimulated and overwhelmed. We just have that wonderful ability to absorb life without the filter others seem to have.

But, in order to function optimally, we have to consciously and purposefully filter out what doesn't serve us. We hear a lot about minimalism nowadays (Marie Kondo again, argh! Leave me alone. I'm keeping my tank tops), but the concept truly does have value. In fact, I would say it amplifies the value of everything in your life! Whether or not you're into underwear origami, less really is more for the sensitive brain.

I wasn't one who knew how to do this instinctively. For a long time, my mindset was more "maximalist" than "minimalist." It's easy to think maximalism equals abundance and minimalism equals scarcity, but it's really quite the opposite.

When we're afraid to say "no" to things or to have less in the way of possessions, we're really in an impoverished place, mentally. We imagine if we don't say "yes" to all the things, we might miss something, disappoint someone, or not have enough. By living in a state of fear (hello again, fight/flight/freeze!), we may find ourselves anxiously grabbing for *things* to ground and cover us.

Being able to say "no" to excess really comes from a place of peace and calm. When we know we are safe and we are enough, it's easier to turn away what may end up weighing us down in the long run. And when we have less to keep track of and maintain, we are more able to enjoy what we do have. In this way, we amplify the value of everything we purposefully choose to keep in our lives.

So for us recovering maximalists, where do we start? As usual, the first step is *noticing*. (Aren't you glad I didn't say the first step is to clean out your closets? Oh, I would never do that to you!)

Where might you be taking on too much, either in possessions or things to do?

Just noticing this helps us slow down and get a bird's eye view of our lives. When we give ourselves that new perspective, we might realize the way we have always done things is not the only (or best) way. Then, we can consciously decide if we want to do things differently.

I realized my brain was definitely not made to handle everything. The more I had to deal with, the more overwhelmed I became. The more I had to do, sort, and organize, the more I spiraled out of control.

I found out (the hard way, as usual) more is not *really* more. I suppose it is more to process, but it doesn't equal more goodness or more results. One thing is for sure: the *more* I say "no" and let go of unnecessary things, the *more* time and energy I have.

It's certainly a continual process, because this world makes the trap of taking on too much *so* tempting. We have to be conscious gatekeepers, turning away things that don't really serve our greater purpose.

Whether it be social engagements, business opportunities, or a tenth pair of ballet flats, all of it can suck our energy and divert our focus. Believe me, I'm also a sucker for the perfect pair of ballet flats, but there is power in being able to say, "What I have is enough."

No matter where in your life you take on too much, I think the quote from author and personal finance coach Nathan W. Morris sums it up nicely: "Edit your life frequently and ruthlessly. It's your masterpiece after all."

Trick #2: Embrace Cycles & Rituals

When it comes to productivity, the power of habits is another thing we hear a lot about—but you know what I've noticed? Highly sensitive, creative, and intuitive people often bristle at the idea of being driven by habits. Some sensitives hate the idea of being boxed into a routine, or doing anything in a monotonous fashion.

What about you? Do you love what habits do for your life, or does the idea of mindlessly doing the same thing, day in and day out, seem like a real drag?

I understand both sides, and personally I've always waffled between the two viewpoints. I understand the benefit of habits, but at the same time find myself rebelling against being boxed in. When I try to create more structure in my life, my brain reacts like a caged feral cat.

If you're also a feral-at-heart HSP, you might benefit from reframing this whole "habits" thing. Perhaps we really are wild, free, untameable creatures of the natural world, but that doesn't mean we should live in a chaotic state. After all, nature isn't chaotic, is it?

We have day and night, seasons, photosynthesis, the water cycle, ocean tides...everything in the natural world is perfectly synchronized in a very predictable dance. What if we could participate in this dance, too?

I don't know about you, but there is something about the idea of being part of nature's symphony that makes my heart go pitter-pat. It feels like getting close to a long lost home.

If you feel like this too, it's no wonder! The natural world was designed with rhythms and cycles to keep everything functioning optimally, and our bodies are encoded with cyclicity as well.

When we struggle against the seeming captivity of habit, we could actually be fighting against our own natural cycles of being. Tuning into the body's cycles, and choreographing our own dance of life around them grounds us. And when we feel grounded, we can move forward with purpose—as opposed to bouncing off the walls like our not-so-friendly feral cat.

More on that in a second, but first, let's consider why highly sensitive people need the structure of "habits" so badly. Our poor brains are already overwhelmed—the last thing we need is more to think about! The beauty of having good habits is once we establish them, we don't have to think about them anymore.

But I know, I know. The word *habit* sounds so boring to some of us. Us creatives prefer to infuse a little extra life into our words, don't we? Personally, the word *ritual* sounds much more inspiring to me than *habit*. It may seem silly to some, but language does matter. Play with phrasing things in a way that resonates with you.

So how do we tune into our natural cycles and create rituals? This could be a whole separate book, but for now, start by noticing your own natural cycles of being. When do you have the most energy and inspiration? When do you need downtime? Consider these questions for your days, months, and even years. (Yes, most of us have times of the year when we feel better than others!) For some this means the winter blues, or Seasonal Affective Disorder, but for many it's more subtle. If you're not sure, consider keeping a journal to help you track your own patterns.

Next, think about those nagging tasks you struggle to get done. Maybe it's exercise, balancing your budget, or working on a creative project. Considering your cycles of mental and physical energy, when the best time is for you to create a ritual for that activity?

For example, a trip to the gym at the time your energy crashes every afternoon is probably not a sustainable ritual. No matter how disciplined or motivated you are, the body is going to win in the end. (Not to mention a crowded gym may be too overstimulating in the first place!) Perhaps a workout at home in the morning or a walk after dinner is more your pace. Forget what other people say is the "right way" to get something done; use your intuition to figure out what works best for *you*.

In the beginning, you're going to need to remind yourself of your new rituals. Write down your intentions to solidify them, set reminders on your phone to free up brain space—oh, and please don't try to begin ten new rituals at once. That's a fine way to get overwhelmed and end up freaking out like a caged feral cat again. This is not a race. One new thing at a time is enough.

Also, remember to make adjustments as necessary. Finding the right flow for your life is a bit of a scientific experiment. Shifting things around and setting aside what doesn't work is part of the process. Eventually, you'll find your groove—and the new rituals will become a familiar part of your dance.

*For a helpful resource on natural cycles, check out author and founder of The Origin Company Kate Northrup. She created the lovely and useful "Do Less Planner" to help you track and maximize your own cyclical energy. Best thing about it? No dates for those of us whose cycles include not using a planner for six months out of the year.

Trick #3: Act on Inspiration

The other morning, I was thinking about things I needed to get done. I was like, "Oh, I really need to juice that kale before it gets wilty. I haven't even washed it yet."

But my little, overthinking brain didn't stop there.

Before long, I realized I was mentally rehearsing *washing kale*, as if somehow by picturing it, the perfect time to physically get off my tush to do it would magically present itself. Why on earth was I imagining prepping greens instead of just walking into the kitchen and getting it done? Sigh. But besides being ridiculous, is there any harm in thinking too much?

As we know, thoughts have real power. Did you know athletes use mental rehearsal as part of their training? In fact, some research has shown muscle strength can be improved with visualization exercises alone![1] Isn't that amazing? "Just thinking" has measurable effects on the body.

Unfortunately, studies have shown kale doesn't get cleaner by visualizing washing it.

When we deeply contemplate something, we may look still, but we are using real energy. No wonder I often feel exhausted before I've gotten anything done! All that thinking is hard work.

HSPs tend to be deep thinkers in addition to our depth of processing unconsciously chugging away in the background. The wonderful thing about this is we are often bursting with inspiration and great ideas. The not-so-wonderful thing is we can get stuck in our own heads, exhausting ourselves before we've taken action.

This thought-inducing exhaustion could be the reason so many of our ideas never come to fruition. Whether it be a burst of creativity or just greens calling out to us from the crisper drawer, if we don't act on our inspiration quickly, things are going to wilt.

Did you know some people don't struggle with this? It's true; there are people who don't procrastinate by overthinking things. They just jump in and do it! Imagine that. My husband is this way, and man, he gets so much done. I'll still be sitting around agonizing over the perfect time and way to complete a task, and he'll be like, "Okay, got that finished. What's next?"

Although we may be naturally lacking this productive impulsiveness, we can still learn to act on inspiration. Years ago I learned a simple trick for this from a presentation by bestselling author and speaker John Maxwell.

He said when you first wake up in the morning, say to yourself, "Do it now" over and over again for about two minutes. You can even make a little song of it.

Do it now, do it now, do it now, do it now, do it now, do it now! This primes your brain for—wait for it—doing things now!

Then, throughout your day, when you think of something to do, say it again: *Do it now, do it now, do it now!*

I'm sure you know what comes next: you actually do things as you think of them instead of waiting for the perfect time (which usually never comes).

Of course, sometimes you honestly can't do a task right now. In that case, write it down. Get it out of your head so it stops sucking energy. I think you'll love how your days flow and how much more you get accomplished when you're acting on inspiration and "doing it now." Thanks, John Maxwell.

Trick #4: Connect Value

When we don't think a task is actually that valuable, we don't feel inspired to follow through with it.

To some people, this sounds ridiculous. After all, if it needs to be done, it needs to be done! Just do it! If you think this way, good for you, but what I've noticed is this: a lot of HSPs and empaths use intuition and feeling as driving forces in our lives. When you have this type of personality, motivation doesn't necessarily come just from seeing what needs to be done. We need to feel emotionally connected to the work.

But hey, this doesn't mean we aren't hard workers! We love to make people happy, which alone usually makes us very conscientious. Honestly, most of us hate the thought of letting others down or having them think less of us. We'll hustle pretty hard to prove ourselves to others, unless it's gotten to where we feel unappreciated no matter what we do. Usually, lack of motivation doesn't strike when others are directly depending on us.

We're more likely to drop the ball when doing so will only disappoint ourselves.

Still, whether working hard for ourselves or others, in order to have the energy to show up consistently and do our best, we need to know we are making an impact. Our drive often comes from intuitively seeing the end result and attaching emotion and meaning to it.

Knowing we are truly adding value, helping someone, and creating something important lights a fire under us.

Thinking like this has its benefits—gives us the impetus to help others and affect change. But it can also give us a bit of a disdain for the mundane tasks of everyday life.

For healers, creatives, inventors, sages, and visionaries, everyday maintenance of our homes, finances, and bodies can feel like time-sucking obstacles between us and our true calling. Yet, we know if we neglect these things they will make an impact on our lives, and not in a good way.

To find motivation to carry on with the business of life, we need to look at what we truly value and want in life. Then, we can figure out how doing what we need to do helps us get what we want most.

Ask yourself: what are your core values in life? I'll tell you a couple of mine: freedom and harmony. I really hate being told what to do, and as a typical empath, I also hate conflict. I know what's important to me, but it can be hard to see how a pile of un-filed paperwork connects with those values. Know what I mean?

So I put it off. The paperwork grows to the size of Mt. Rushmore. I continue to ignore it, thinking I have bigger fish to fry. It gets to the point where I'm breaking out in a cold sweat at the idea of needing to find a receipt, because God only knows where it could be. I dig through the paper mountain in a mad panic, praying for divine intervention and swearing I'm going to get my life together after this. Once the crisis has passed, I stuff the paper mountain in a cardboard box and carry on with my life until the next critical situation arises. Rinse and repeat.

Were our highly sensitive, empathic brains designed for such nonsense as junk mail and filing receipts? Probably not. If you were born to a tribe in the rainforest, you'd probably be healing people with native plants and doing just fine with keeping track of life. Some aspects of modern existence are not in our wheelhouse, but we really are capable of doing these things when we need to. We just have to reframe them in a way where we clearly see their value.

Let's look at how I could do this in order to conquer Paperwork Mountain. First, I could notice how my core value of freedom plays in. After all, if I am organized, I can better attend to matters of finance. I remember the wisdom of the Proverb: "The borrower is a slave to the lender."[2] Ugh. I hate the idea of being a slave! That really hits a nerve and lights a fire under me.

By being organized with papers, I can know where financial documents are. I'm not in danger of losing money because I can't find receipts. By managing finances wisely, I create more freedom for our family to stay out of debt and do the things that are important to us.

I also create harmony, because my husband isn't going to be irritated that I forgot to pay a bill or put the current insurance certificate in the car. I have more inner harmony, because I'm not nervous about having forgotten or lost something important. Thinking about it this way, I feel more compelled to change the way I've been doing things. Instead of feeling overwhelmed about it and shutting down, my mind starts to put together a plan.

Can you see how this works? We aren't putting the business of life off because we can't do it. We just need to see the long term impact to feel motivated. When a task resonates with your core values, you will find a way to make it happen.

Whew—I've thrown a lot at you in this chapter. Our tendency when reading is to say, "Oh, yeah, good idea," then forty-eight hours later, we've forgotten about it—so, if you struggle with organization and productivity, pick just *one* suggestion in this chapter to try this week. There is space in the journal to hash out your plan. Then, mark this chapter and set a reminder on your phone to choose another tip to experiment with next week.

Remember, none of this is a race! Let go of the impulse to do it all at once or not at all. Choose to believe that where you are right now is just where you are supposed to be at the moment. The lessons you have learned so far will all help you on your journey forward.

Keep taking small steps forward, and before you know it, you'll be amazed at how far you've come. Still, sometimes we have setbacks. Things can happen beyond our control, pushing us into overwhelm and making us feel like we're back at square one. In the next chapter, we'll talk about how to keep going and upgrade our resilience no matter what life throws at us.

---

1. Hynes, Janette & Turner, Zach. (2020). Positive Visualization and Its Effects on Strength Training. Impulse.
2. "Proverbs 22:7" Essay. In New World Translation of the Holy Scriptures: Rendered from the Original Languages. Brooklyn, NY: Watchtower Bible and Tract Society of New York, Inc., 2013.

Chapter 16

Resilience 2.0

"We need to sit on the rim of the well of darkness and fish for fallen light with patience." --- Pablo Neruda[1]

I thought I was resilient until moving and mold toxicity taxed my system. I thought I was resilient until my child got really sick. I thought I was resilient until March 2020 had me obsessively taking in information about COVID-19 along with carbs and wine.

I think we all have our "I thought I was resilient until..." stories. Each of us, at one time or another, finds ourselves on the slippery edge of the well of darkness, not sure how we are going to find the light again. What about you? Have you ever felt like you finally had your act together, only to be completely derailed by one thing or another? Maybe the events of a certain year (or even *years)* have left you reeling in the dark?

If you're struggling, know you aren't alone.

Whilst in the midst or aftermath of an intense experience, it's easy to get down on ourselves. We may think, "Man, I should really be able to handle this better!" Perhaps, feeling beat up and exhausted, we might wonder if we aren't so resilient after all.

Well, my friend, being resilient doesn't mean you'll never get knocked on your butt. Resilient people can still get depressed. Sometimes we all feel maxed out and struggle just to put one foot in front of the other. It isn't just you.

We all have our own unique capacity for handling stress. This capacity is shaped by our biology, our history, and the state of our nervous systems. And as we've learned, just having a sensitive nervous system affects how we handle stress, because we're already absorbing more than most. No matter how mentally strong we are or how hard we try, sometimes circumstances are going to push us past our breaking point.

When this happens to you, it doesn't mean you've failed in some way. It just means you're a human being living through some very tough things. And as a human, you also have the capacity for developing greater resilience—meaning, you *can* bounce back when life knocks you down.

If you're thinking, "Umm...I'm not exactly bouncing," I get it. One reason we sometimes fail to bounce back is because we live in stressful times. It's hard to recover from stress when the stress just keeps coming!

As we talked about in previous chapters, our poor little adrenal glands can get "fried" from pumping out stress hormones. When stress keeps pounding us, our guts can't rest and digest, and our nervous systems get stuck in fight/flight/freeze responses. Even if you *know* all the things in this book, you can still feel decidedly unable to bounce. Yes, I've been there, too.

Let's dive a little deeper into five specific challenges highly sensitive people face during tumultuous times, as well as how we can continue to upgrade our resilience despite them.

#1 Loss of Routine

I think most people, sensitive and empathic or not, like to feel in control of their lives. I know I do. For highly sensitive people, a natural coping mechanism is to control our environment in order to avoid feeling overwhelmed. So, when we suddenly find ourselves in situations that are completely out of our control, it can really shake us to the core.

We all need time to recover from upsets, but when something crazy is going on, we may not be able to catch a break. Forget about upsetting the apple cart—the cart is turned over, smashed to bits, and all the apples have rolled into the street.

When things have spun out of control, it's easy just to go with the frantic energy—and once we're in it, it sure is hard to pull ourselves out. So, how can we keep ourselves grounded when our whole life seems to be upended?

Perhaps there are no easy answers, but we might take some comfort in setting up little rituals throughout the day. Maybe it's five minutes of stretching or prayer in the morning, a ten minute walk at the same time every day, or reading a chapter of a book or journaling before bed. Maybe it's just stepping out in the fresh air and doing some breathing exercises, noticing the natural world. You get the idea. Give yourself little gifts of time to reorient and find bits of joy amidst the chaos.

#2 Emotional Conflict

When we're stressed, all our weak points start bubbling to the surface, don't they? C'mon, I know it's not just me. This is especially noticeable during collectively stressful experiences, because everyone is a mess at once. It can get ugly real quick.

The day before the COVID-19 pandemic lockdowns started, people were getting into fist fights at Sam's Club. I'm guessing those people weren't highly sensitive or empaths, as we probably are less likely to hit fellow shoppers over the head with items from our grocery carts. No, we HSPs are more prone to *emotional* conflicts than physical ones—and unfortunately, emotional conflicts (AKA arguments) are oh-so-easy to come by, these days.

Like many of us, I have always enjoyed deep discussions, so it has kind of taken me off guard how quickly conversation now deteriorates into conflict. Almost every topic has a polarized, emotional charge to it—and of course, social media brings it to a whole new level. Who would have thought we'd someday carry around tiny computers we could use to argue with other people without ever actually seeing or speaking to them?

Anyway, trying to engage in a meaningful conversation nowadays feels a lot like poking a crocodile. I think this is especially hard for our visionary types, who really *want* to poke the crocodile. We're very passionate people who look at the world differently from most. Because of our big picture thinking and strong intuition, we tend to see things coming sooner than others—and they tend to think we're criminally insane for it (only *halfway* joking there).

As visionaries, we might feel it's our responsibility to help others see what we see. The Martin Luther King Jr. quote, "Our lives begin to end the day we become silent about things that matter," may resonate deeply for us, in times like these.

It's no surprise if we feel called to educate others about one thing or another, but while we really can't shut up about the things that matter, we also have to use wisdom as to when is the time to speak and who we are going to engage with.

We already know getting into arguments is extremely draining for us sensitives, because it's not just over when the conversation ends. Instead, the residual negative energy can feel trapped in our bodies. Who else has experienced a nervous system hangover? I sure have had my share of lively discussions and post-argument migraines to show for them.

So, when is it worth it to engage, and when is it not? If it's going to make you physically ill, the answer is: "Do not engage, I repeat, do not engage!"

Even knowing how much it's going to drain you, the pull to defend your perspective is strong, isn't it? At this point, it can be helpful to consider our motives before we jump into the fray. I often have to ask myself, "Um, do I really want to help someone, or do I just want them to see that I'm right?" And I say this as someone who *really* enjoys being right.

While we may think it's helpful, is it really our responsibility to correct someone else's "wrong" thinking? Not really. They are in charge of their own brains, and their own decisions.

It *is,* however, our personal responsibility to take care of our own health and protect our own energy.

Besides, I've noticed (and maybe you've realized it too) people rarely change their minds, and they *never* do so when they are in an emotional state (like, in an argument). When someone is worked up into fight or flight, it doesn't matter how much logic you present or science glitter you sprinkle on them. When in a state of fear or anger, the part of the brain that would process such information is no longer engaged. As much as it's tempting to try, you might as well be poking a crocodile for how well it's going to turn out.

Engage in conversations when both you and the other person are on a calm wavelength. Never when in a prickly, "I'm right, you're wrong," ego-protective mode. And arguing with strangers on the internet? You know your time and energy are worth more than that.

Oh, I know, you still want to argue. And perhaps sometimes you should. I get it. But please, make it a priority to protect your energy, health, and peace. Choose your battles wisely. I once heard it said there are some battles that aren't meant to be won, but are meant to be survived. You have to figure out the difference for yourself. But remember, no one benefits from you burning out and going down in a blaze of glory.

#3 Absorbing Outside Pain

For empaths particularly, it may feel natural to carry the weight of the world on our shoulders. Soul and body crushing, but natural nonetheless. After all, our sensitive healer type is so good at caring for people during tumultuous times. This is a beautiful thing, but also a heavy load to carry.

As empaths, we don't just *notice* other people's pain. To one extent or another, depending on how attuned we are, we feel it in our own bodies. And as we learned in Chapter 5, this can happen both physically and emotionally.

When someone we love is hurting or depressed, we just wish we could fix it. Not only because we love them, of course, but honestly because we'd really like to stop feeling their pain, too! It may seem a little selfish, but it's just part of the messy experience of feeling things outside of yourself.

As if all that wasn't enough, some empathic people also are affected by *collective* energy. I'm sure that sounds super weird to some, but really, we all feel other people's "vibes." Just think of walking into a room where there has been some sort of drama going on. You can feel it, can't you? Hence the expression, "you could cut the tension with a knife."

Our bodies recognize the electromagnetic energy fields around us, even if some of our minds poo-poo it. It only makes sense that this would be true on a large scale, as well. If the majority of people are feeling very tense about something, that heavy energy is out there—and palpable to those who are more sensitive.

Have you noticed this yourself? I realized the power of collective energy myself when I noticed how motivated and energized I am when school is starting back up. Even though public school has zero effect on my family's schedule, I still get a sense of excitement every year. Funny, huh?

Collective energy is wonderful when it's positive, but when times get tough, the heaviness in the air can feel like you're slogging through a swamp. Being alive during the COVID-19 era we have felt the unique weight of worldwide bad news. This can also happen on a smaller scale, perhaps with a disappointing announcement like pay cuts or the loss of a big contract at the office. If you're struggling with this, notice where the energy is coming from. It may not seem very productive, but just becoming aware of why we feel so weighed down is a great first step.

Remember the tools you've learned. Visualize yourself pushing the negative energy away or gently handing it back to the person it came from. When we're feeling all the feelings outside of us, usually we're very disconnected from our own feelings and our own bodies. Practicing being present in ourselves is *so* important.

To do this, feel your feet on the ground or the pressure of the chair against your backside. Scan your body for discomfort. Do you need to move around? Or is the body trying to tell you something else?

For example, I often notice I'm putting all my weight on one foot —brilliantly, the one that hurts all the time! For another example, when my mind is spinning, the molecules of emotion are going crazy in my gut (ouch). But as I slow my mind down and let myself feel the sensations in my belly, the discomfort starts to dissipate. It might be different for you; just tune in and see what happens.

If you aren't in any pain, that's good! Just practice feeling where your body is, noticing your breath, engaging your physical senses, and calmly taking in the environment around you. Doing this regularly can help remind our empathic selves what is really ours and what isn't.

#4 Obsessing Over Things Outside of Our Control

We've always known life is full of uncertainty, but most people function by not thinking too much about the unknowns. We have our little plans and tell ourselves it's all going to work out. When something comes along that flips our proverbial apple cart, it's easy to panic.

How am I going to pick up all these apples? How am I going to fix my cart? In reality, these questions are more like, Am I going to find a new job? Am I going to be able to pay the rent? Is civil unrest going to affect me? Is the person I love going to be OK? When is this going to be over? Is it going to happen again?

We all hate uncertainty. Having your life turned upside down is certainly not easy for anyone, but it can really tax an already sensitive nervous system. When you're just waiting for the other shoe to drop, you aren't exactly resting and digesting, are you? As humans, we just want to know we and our loved ones are going to be OK. Not knowing can leave our entire bodies on edge, unable to properly function or heal.

The visionary type has an additional layer of challenge here. Not only do we visionaries want to know we'll be alright, we also kind of want to know if the whole world will be alright. The visionary is driven to see the big picture and understand why things are happening the way they are. Oh, and we're good at it too. If there's information to be found, we'll find it. We know how to hold all the possibilities in our heads until the puzzle pieces fall together—or our heads explode, one or the other.

This magnetic pull to unearth hidden truths isn't something we can just turn off, nor would we want to. If you have that drive, it's part of what makes you *you*. However, it is wise to consider when our need to make sense of things becomes an obsession.

Personally, I tend to go whole hog when it comes to taking in information. I want to understand it all, and I want to understand it now. This is particularly the case when I'm sensing uncertainty and topsy turviness in my world. I don't know about you, but part of me thinks if I can just wrap my head around the situation, everything will be OK again. Except then I do, and it still isn't.

We can't always make things right, and we don't always (or ever) really know exactly how things will turn out. I recently read *Loving What Is* by Byron Katie. While I didn't agree with everything (because I'm still a control freak perhaps), it really did help calm my little squirrel brain.

One of the things Katie talks about is "being in God's business."[2] I realize not everyone who reads this will share a belief in God, but highly sensitive people are usually pretty spiritually aware. Most of us know there is more going on than what we can see with our little human eyeballs.

Anyway, it resonated with me that sometimes, in obsessing over things outside of my control, I am just poking around in God's business. It's not my job to know everything or fix everything. I may not like giving up control, but in reality I never had control in the first place.

Sometimes, obsessive information seeking is simply a distraction from grief. When bad things happen, it's hard to accept it as our current reality. We think, "This can't be happening. It's not supposed to happen this way. I had so many plans..." We figure that maybe, if we can figure out why it happened, we can fix it. And if we can hurry up and fix it, we don't ever have to stop and feel the emotional tidal wave rising in our bodies. So we shove our feelings down and get to work on a plan to alter reality.

Well, you remember what happens to those zombie emotions, right? Even if it turns out we can change the tide on something, we still have to allow ourselves to feel and process those molecules of emotion. To move forward in a healthy way, we need to grieve what needs to be grieved, and let go of what is beyond our control.

Let's face it though: we're intense people, and maybe we kind of need something to obsess over. Take away our ability to *do something*, and we're likely to end up feeling very stuck. So, if you're in the position to do so, why not give yourself something that is in your control to obsess over?

Maybe it's finally starting that side business, writing a book, or working on your art again. It could be learning how to grow your own food or medicinal herbs. We can't control everything, but we can choose which things within our realm of responsibility to focus our energy on. And sometimes the best thing we can do for the macrocosm is to get our microcosm in order.

Still, we have to realize a dysregulated nervous system isn't necessarily able to get on board with such projects. Sometimes, as much as we want to focus on things that are healthy and productive, we're just really, truly feeling stuck. It's legitimate, and doesn't mean you aren't trying hard enough. It also doesn't mean you're broken or going to be stuck forever. Which brings us to our last-but-not-least topic...

#5 Getting Stuck in Nervous System Dysregulation

If you're feeling stuck, you aren't alone. Remember when I told you about my bit-of-rock-bottom experience? When it happened, I felt numbed out, lacking in creativity and motivation, disconnected from my body and the world around me. Oh, and I gained a ton of weight. Not being able to wear your favorite jeans just adds insult to injury, doesn't it?

Some might write this off as "depression," which sounds fair enough. But there was more to it, as is so often the case. I knew pretty plainly that my nervous system was overwhelmed, and thought I'd recover once things calmed down. But the stress just kept on coming (life again, right?) No matter how hard I tried to implement healthy habits, I just felt the same—or worse. I really didn't understand the full extent of it at the time.

By now, we all know a bit about the autonomic nervous system and how stress affects our overall well-being. Once again, there's that state of low-level, constant fight or flight. When we're in this state, we might be anxious and hypervigilant. We're always a bit on edge, and we can't properly digest and heal. Then there's the third state that can become activated: *freeze*.

To understand freeze, think of that furry little critter called the opossum whose defense mechanism is to appear dead. Opossums do this really well, with their lips turning black and mouth foaming for an extra touch of drama. Other animals, including humans, also have a protective immobility response built into their parasympathetic nervous systems, though for us, it's thankfully just a bit more subtle.

When humans go into freeze mode, our heart rate decreases, blood goes to the core, and oxygen and metabolism both go down. Along with this, we experience numbness and dissociation (meaning feeling detached from your body and environment), which are really brilliant responses designed to protect us from pain.

Of course, while this immobility system is necessary to have on board for shock trauma and injury, our bodies aren't supposed to stay stuck in it. But when we have long term stress and can't sustain fight or flight anymore, our systems are forced to use freeze as a conservation mode.

If this has happened to you, you might feel like the electricity is out in your body, and you're trying to run everything on a tiny generator. You're just keeping the necessities online and everything else is a lost cause. Trying to access your creativity in freeze mode? Forget about it.

Dissociation from one's body really takes a toll. Have you ever seen the original *Men in Black* movie? Remember the alien cockroach awkwardly traipsing around in the human suit? After being disconnected from your body long enough, that's kind of how it feels.

Whose body is this, and how do I move it? At least for me, when I am dissociating, I can't feel much of anything in my body except for pain from moving the wrong way for too long. Not a good feeling. If your own body feels a bit alien to you, it's possible you're also stuck in freeze mode.

Anyone's nervous system can become dysregulated and stuck, but highly sensitive people may be more susceptible to getting maxed out—and if you had a rough start with early childhood trauma, this is all the more likely.

If you relate to this and are feeling a little distraught about opossums foaming at the mouth and alien roaches, sorry about that. I can't resist a really unpleasant and overly dramatic visual.

Anyway, what I really want you to know is this: all your body wants is to keep you safe and sound.

The nervous system is always looking for clues that it's OK to rest and heal, but sometimes the conditions in our world make it difficult to find that sense of safety and keep our systems regulated. After all, we may be dealing with unsafe situations and have legitimate reasons to be fearful. So, what do we do?

First of all, cut yourself some slack. It's kind of scary in itself to find your inner electricity is flickering. We might worry about what others will think of us, or wonder if we have what it takes to keep up with this life. Know that you are not lazy or unmotivated just because you have slowed down. Your body is quite likely just in conservation mode—and as I've said before, you can't undo the damage from stress by punishing yourself with more stress. Let go of the high expectations. You are a human *being*, not a human *doing*. You are every bit as worthy in this state as you are in your top form.

Still, we don't want to stay stuck forever, and there are things we need to do to take care of ourselves and our families. Whatever is going on outside of us, we need to keep working on regulating our systems, getting back "into" our bodies, and building our capacity for handling stressful situations.

While being aware of what's going on with our sensitive selves is a good first step, a dysregulated nervous system is something we'll probably need some help to recover from. As I mentioned in Chapter 9, somatic experiencing is a great tool for nervous system rescue and recovery.

So, which of the five things sensitive people struggle with during stressful times did you relate to most? Loss of routine, emotional conflict, absorbing outside pain, obsessing over things outside your control, or perhaps full-on nervous system dysregulation? Maybe (eek!) all of the above?

If you're feeling this chapter, I invite you to take a few minutes to journal about what you're dealing with right now. You can use the prompts in the free journal. Haven't downloaded it yet? It's almost the end of the book, what are you waiting for?

And please, give yourself a pat on the back for what you are doing well, despite all the craziness. If you're currently in the midst of an intense situation, do what you can, get help when you can, and give yourself lots of grace. No matter what is going on in your world, always remember that you and your gifts are needed. You are never alone. Keep going.

---

1. Neruda, Pablo, and William O'Daly. The Sea and the Bells. Copper Canyon Press, 2002.
2. Katie, Byron, and Stephen Mitchell. Loving What Is. Harmony Books, 2002.

Chapter 17

Three Secret Keys

*"Do you know what you are? You are a manuscript of a divine letter. You are a mirror reflecting a noble face. The universe is not outside of you. Look inside yourself; everything that you want, you are already that." ---
Rumi*

Throughout this book, we've talked a lot about building resilience, so, we probably already know what the word means! Still, I thought it was interesting that one of the definitions of resilience is "the power or ability to return to the original form, position, etc., after being bent, compressed, or stretched; elasticity."[1]

I would venture to say that as humans, our resilience does not involve returning to our original form. We can never be, and are not meant to be, the same. What stretches us launches us forward. What compresses us pulls from deep within our strength to break out.

We are not the same after this process; we are stronger. With a few more wrinkles and gray hairs, perhaps, but still, *stronger*. Resilience isn't something we have; it's something we *are*. It's a gift programmed into all of our cells. Resilience is innate in each of us. We just have to learn to access what is already there: the human ability to heal and grow.

I hope this book has helped you access more of your own inner power and claim what's been yours all along. Everything I've written here is just a mirror, just words to reflect back all the lovely angles you might not have seen in yourself.

When we tend to stand out as different from most, we may not get a lot of positive affirmation. It can leave us wondering if there's something wrong with us. I hope you've come to see how much is right with you, as a highly sensitive soul.

Of course, being sensitive and empathic doesn't mean we're perfect or somehow better than any other person. We've also talked about some ways we get tripped up (people-pleasing, people fixing, etcetera, etcetera). We aren't angels by any means, and that's OK, too.

Being this way is a gift—one that's very much rooted in how our nervous systems are wired. Since having a regulated nervous system is so pivotal to health and well-being, we need to take extra good care of ourselves. Constant powering through and pretending to be a machine can destroy our health from the inside out.

Hopefully, you've gained some new insight into living with a highly sensitive nervous system. It isn't always going to be easy, but it still can be wonderful.

Deep down inside, you already are who you were made to be. Your sensitive gifts have never left you—they are in your DNA! It's our trauma responses, habits, and emotional patterns that keep us stuck behaving in ways that don't serve our true selves.

So, let's wrap this book up with three keys to help you unlock your own resilience. Consider this a little treasure map to guide you on your journey.

Secret Key #1: Accepting Yourself

I recently saw a meme that I loved. It simply said, "I am the glitch in the Matrix." Laugh all you want, but I'm happy to be the glitch! I don't usually fit in, and I'm OK with that. To me, "the Matrix" is just that which isn't as it appears to be on the surface, and highly sensitive people are generally not surface dwellers.

Visionary types are basically anything but surface dwellers. Diving deep is just how our brains function. The surface is one place where I personally have not felt accepted by most.

How about you? Your experience may be different from mine, but there are probably some ways in which you feel misunderstood. Maybe you've hidden or shrunk part of yourself to fit in. You might even hold a bit of resentment about how difficult it is to be highly sensitive.

In order to grow and stop subjecting ourselves to the "fit into the box" contortions, we need to accept our true selves (whether anyone else does or not). It's a balancing act, because while we shouldn't feel inferior for being ourselves, protecting our egos with delusions of superiority isn't healthy either. We can love and accept where we are (with humility) while still honoring where others are, too.

After all, everyone has their own gifts, and each individual is in a different place. They don't have to understand for you to be OK, and you don't have to be angry, frustrated, or hurt about their lack of understanding, either.

I know being misunderstood can be a frustrating and painful experience. I've felt all of those molecules of emotion and then some, but a new layer of realization I've come to is that people don't have to understand me. I don't have to explain myself. They can misunderstand me all day; I am still the same person, with or without their stamp of approval.

We all want to feel understood, but those who are not on the same path as you probably can't see what you see, no matter how well you describe it, or how logical or obvious it seems. But it also doesn't matter if they think you are nuts.

From their viewpoint, things look different, so isn't it silly to waste our time and energy wishing they would validate what we see?

You see what you see, and you know what you know. It's enough. Learn to enjoy the view.

Once again, accepting yourself isn't an act of ego inflation. It's just deciding to be at peace with reality. This is who you are, and it's OK. You are safe, lovable, and enough. And so are the people who don't get you.

I know the ego wants to go "but, but, BUT..." Quiet the mental chatter, and let yourself feel the peace that comes with acceptance. I think you'll like it.

Trying to control people's perceptions of us and contorting ourselves to fit it in takes a lot of energy, doesn't it? However, the more we can live in that peaceful place of acceptance, the more our bodies will be able to rest and heal.

This brings us to our second key:

Secret Key #2: Protect Your Energy

By now, we all understand why being highly sensitive and empathic feels so exhausting: because processing everything so deeply is, legit, a lot of work! We talked about it in the "No & Yes" chapter, but it bears repeating: we have to constantly be our own loving caregivers and give a firm "no" to the things that drain us.

Always be mindful of how your nervous system is reacting to your situation. We do this by checking in with how the body is responding.

Is there tension or tightness? Knots in the stomach? A surge of emotion followed by numbness? These are all little clues your body is giving you, clues we might tune out as we spin our thoughts or indulge in our sensory addiction of choice.

The more we stop and listen to our bodies, the more space we can create to choose something different. And the more often we say "yes" to what we really need and "no" to what we don't, the more energy we'll have for the things that matter most.

A huge energy drain for me has been emotional addiction. With emotional addiction, our bodies crave the "hit" of neurotransmitters that are released when we experience strong emotion. Surprisingly, the emotions we become addicted to are often miserable ones, like anger, indignation, or sadness.

When we're emotionally addicted, it feels uncomfortable just to be *still*. It's like there's a war going on in the nervous system, going back and forth between feeling triggered and upset and feeling exhausted and numb, with no in-between. We end up seeking out a charge of strong emotion just to feel *something*. Have you ever felt emotionally addicted? It's easy to get off-kilter with our emotions when the world turns into a looney bin, huh?

Once again, there is so much value in just being aware of what we are doing and what's happening in our bodies—like, "Oh, here I am, starting an argument again," or, "Here I am, staring at my phone again, trying to find something to annoy me." Instead of ramping up our negative emotions or numbing out, we can drop back into our bodies and feel what is really going on.

Because guess what? Your sensitive nervous system feels a lot safer when you are present in your body. That safety begets healing, and a healed body is an energized body. This is an oversimplified explanation, but I think it's a good place to start.

So start paying attention to your physical body. As empaths, we often know what others are feeling more than we know what we ourselves are feeling. We do more to keep others well than we do for ourselves.

So, what can you commit to begin doing today to take care of your body? What does your body really want for fuel? What kind of movement are you craving?

Of course, movement is life, but pushing yourself to do something extremely challenging, mind-over-matter style, is probably not the best first step for your nervous system. Those of us who have a disconnection from the body built into our survival toolbox have to make those connections to be present and feel where we are in space first, before anything else.

Reclaiming your energy may seem complicated, but it shouldn't be—especially since complexity is exhausting. If you're like me and can wear yourself out just with your own complex thinking, you know exactly what I mean. Say "yes" to something today that gives you energy, and say "no" to something that drains you. Over time, I think you'll find these little steps in the right direction have moved you to beautiful new places.

And after that, unlocking the next door may come quite naturally...

Secret Key #3: Do Your Work

Everyone—highly sensitive and empathic or not—has their own secret sauce, their own special recipe that makes them uniquely and wonderfully *themselves*. We're comparing it to a treasure hunt, but here's the thing: you don't have to go very far to find it. It's always been inside you. You just have to start digging.

So often, we learn to hide what makes us unique—we do this because we felt awkward or different or undervalued, or it just so happened that we buried our gifts under more pressing matters. In any case, many of us have lost touch with the things that make us feel like ourselves—and it doesn't feel good to go through life not truly being yourself, does it?

So, why spend another day not being you?

Don't skim over this next question. Humor me, and really answer it: What is one small thing you could do every day to feel more like your true self?

Maybe it's writing, painting, playing music, inventing? Hint: it isn't laundry. But really, I don't need to give you any hints on how to figure this out. You already know. Everybody knows, at the core of their being, what they are supposed to be doing. They often just haven't given themselves permission to follow through with it (yet).

Perhaps some of you are thinking, "No, wait, I really don't know! I have no idea what I'm supposed to be doing! Can someone tell me what I should do?"

Nope.

I'm afraid no one else can tell you but yourself. Keep listening. Your intuition already knows. Maybe you just have to do a little more reconnecting with yourself before you can hear it, but you will hear it someday.

Of course, once we embrace the realization of what we should be doing and commit to doing it, we'd love for it to be smooth sailing. Woohoo, it's like you're king of the world, smelling that salty sea air of self-actualization! And next thing you know, you're hitting a giant iceberg.

Such is life. If doing what you love were easy in this world, everyone would be doing it. Sometimes time and energy drains trip us up, but we can also fall under the pressure we put on ourselves to be productive and only do things we excel at.

After all, when you dig up your talents after burying them for years, they're going to be rusty. In fact, whatever secret sauce you're cooking up, there's a good chance it's going to stink before it can sparkle.

And no doubt, it will be frustrating to think of where you'd be if you'd never buried those gifts. Trust me, I know. Don't get me started on how long it's taken me to be able to write again. At first, it felt like I had to excavate every word from the dark and mostly empty caverns of my brain. Sometimes, it still does.

Once upon a time, I was also pretty good at drawing. Now my art looks worse than it did when I was twelve. Working on it is a humbling practice for sure. But no matter how dopey-looking a piece comes out, allowing my forty-something-year-old self to be creative helps heal the inner child, who is still in there somewhere.

We have to begin our work as an act of healing, not as an act of productivity. Allow yourself to grieve for what was lost, then, try embracing the idea that right now, you are exactly where you are supposed to be.

And for Pete's sake, stop pressuring yourself to make money with your gifts. In time, it may come. There is plenty of room for the possibility that your talents will bring you financial abundance. But you have to do your time healing, *first*.

Once you commit to working on your unique gifts, you'll probably find a million reasons why you should be doing something else, instead. There will be business opportunities. People asking for your help with their projects. Messes to be cleaned up.

Like right now, I'm feeling really drawn to cleaning the oven. And I've cleaned an oven less than ten times in my entire life, so obviously, it isn't that important to me!

Notice your own patterns of avoidance. For another example, I've often sat down to write only to find myself inexplicably drawn to browsing cat condos on Amazon. Why? Do I have a very demanding kitty?

No. I only have a semi-demanding kitty.

What's really stopping me is actually *resistance*, the phenomenon famously brought to light in writer Steven Pressfield's book, *The War of Art*. Resistance lives in the nervous system. It doesn't yet feel comfortable doing what you need to do, so it says, "Hey, let's organize the spice cabinet, instead!"

Alphabetizing your cinnamon and smoked paprika is safe. Doing your art is risky. Art (and any other new endeavor) opens you up to the possibility of experiencing criticism, failure, rejection, and a whole bunch of other unpleasant feelings you had in the past. And in that moment of decision, it seems almost impossible to do anything but give in to the resistance.

Of course, you won't give up forever. Just for today. You'll do your art tomorrow. Except tomorrow ends up the same way, and so does the next day, and the cycle of procrastination continues for years upon years until it seems too late.

Perhaps until it really is too late.

Succumbing to resistance doesn't feel good. We aren't doing what we know we should be doing, we end up carrying around a heavy, anxious feeling that saps our energy.

And so, we must lean into the fight, day after day. We must continually coax ourselves to do just a little bit more of what our souls simultaneously crave and fear, and slowly, our nervous systems will start to acclimate and our bodies will feel at home again. It can feel like slogging through quicksand, but it does get better. We just have to keep going.

Remember, working on your secret sauce is not a selfish endeavor. We need you to be you! The gift you've been hiding may be the key someone else needs in their life.

Of course, when you begin to step into your true identity, there will be some people who ain't likin' it. The tribe may want to put you back in what they perceive as "your place." As empaths, this disappointment can be hard to deal with. We may feel the pull to stop what we're doing and preserve a more peaceful-feeling status quo, but in the long term, doing so would leave us feeling anything but peaceful.

We can't filter our lives through the lens of outside approval. No human being is an expert on your life except *you*. Your responsibility to others is to be kind, honest, and ethical. It isn't to pretend to be just like them, trapped in an echo chamber of sameness. You may lose connection with some people along the way, but you'll also find ones who love and support you, no matter what.

In Closing

In one final, awkward confession, I'll tell you this: much of my time on this planet has been spent semi-desperately looking for some way or something to *fix* my highly sensitive self. A supplement to give me the body of a stronger, more athletic person. A course from an expert to tell me what I'm doing wrong. A book to tell me how to just act normal and do normal things!

Some things I've experimented with have added value, but many have not. Mostly what I've found is this: *I had what I needed all along.* The best tools I've found were ones that taught me how to tap into what I already possessed.

I hope this book has done a little of that for you. As a highly sensitive and empathic person, you already have the building blocks of resilience in your DNA. You have unique and amazing gifts no one can take away from you.

All you have to do is take hold of what you've had all along.

I can't wait to see what you make of it.

---

1. "Resilience Definition & Meaning." Dictionary.com. Dictionary.com. Accessed November 3, 2021. https://www.dictionary.com/browse/resilience.

A note before you go...

Would you do me a quick favor? If you found this book valuable, will you leave a review on Amazon or Goodreads? It will take under a minute and would really help get this book into the hands of more empaths and HSPs. Thank you from the bottom of my electromagnetic heart!

I truly appreciate you reading this book. But let's not say goodbye forever! If you'd like to keep in touch and hear about upcoming books and new resources for HSPs, sign up for emails at: www.jenniferlaurenparker.com

You can also find me on Instagram at: jenniferlaurenparker

Acknowledgements

I'd like to acknowledge my family, especially my husband, for supporting me in my endeavors. Even when they seem crazy. Even when my ambitious streak combined with lack of time urgency results in you not being able to find matching socks. I appreciate you.

Thank you to all three of my boys. I am so proud of the kind, sensitive, intelligent, and strong humans you are growing up to be.

Thanks to my mom for always being there and for talking me off quite a few proverbial ledges.

Thanks to all the friends who get my weirdness and keep me sane. You know who you are.

A special thank you to the talented Owen B Shots for taking my author photo.

Thank you to my editor (who shall remain anonymous in case I messed anything up after she worked so hard.) I appreciate you understanding my humor.

Thank you to artist Paula Ambrosio for answering my query on 99 Designs. I am so grateful for you envisioning something so perfect for the subject. The cover is more lovely than I could have imagined!

And a big thank you to the Self Publishing School community for walking me through this process. Without your input I might have ended up with a title and cover that had people wondering if this is a book about cooking elephants. Ha!

I also can't neglect to acknowledge Lauren Roxburgh and her Aligned Life Studio foam roller workouts. Because tech-neck and shoulders are real.

Finally, thanks to all of you who are reading this book. I appreciate you more than you know.

Sincerely, Jennifer

About the Author

Jennifer is a certified Health & Life Coach and Aroma Freedom Technique Practitioner. When she's not writing, Jennifer enjoys pondering the mysteries of the universe, making people laugh, and hanging out with her husband, three boys, and two fur babies. If she isn't at home, she's probably out for a walk or at the local nursery looking for just one more plant.

Made in the USA
Middletown, DE
28 May 2024

55003812R00118